HAUNTED JONESBOROUGH

Charles Edwin Price

Cover Art and Design by David Dixon

The Overmountain Press

JOHNSON CITY, TENNESSEE

Other books by Charles Edwin Price

Haints, Witches and Boogers:
Tales from Upper East Tennessee

Demon In The Woods:
Tall Tales and True From East Tennessee

The Mystery of Ghostly Vera
And Other Haunting Tales of Southwest Virginia

The Day They Hung The Elephant

ISBN 0-932807-93-3

2 3 4 5 6 7 8 9 0

Dedicated to the Memory of

Paul M. Fink
(1892-1980)

For all he did to chronicle
Washington County History and Folklore

Introduction

Many tourists in upper East Tennessee feel they've missed out on something very special unless they visit Jonesborough, a small farming community located about 10 miles south of Johnson City. Like the ghosts that populate the town and surrounding countryside, Jonesborough, too, rose from the dead. Today, Jonesborough is a flourishing tourist attraction, saved from the ravages of neglect by far-sighted business people.

By the 1960s, Jonesborough was nearly a ghost town. Most of its business was snatched away by modern shopping centers in nearby Johnson City. To save itself, the town shifted gears. Specialty shops, antique stores, boutiques, and fine restaurants bloomed along Main Street. Restoration of the downtown historic district gave the town a much needed face-lift.

Sue Henley, a Washington County native, and her husband, Gerald, are co-owners of The Cherry Tree, a craft shop located on Main Street. She remembers, as a child, coming to Jonesborough every Saturday afternoon with her family to shop—a ritual in those days when most of the business had not yet moved away to Johnson City.

And she was also there at the beginning of Jonesborough's renaissance, years later. "When I moved into town, Jonesborough was just a ghost town," she told me recently. "There was not three or four viable businesses in this whole town. The pharmacy was there. Lavender's (a food store) was there. But there were not enough businesses here to warrant people coming to Jonesborough. There was just no reason to come to Jonesborough."

Sue, who is very active in the Jonesborough Civic Trust, credits Jonesborough historian Paul Fink as being one of the shining lights behind Jonesborough's revitalization. She also credits Jimmy Neil Smith, former Jonesborough mayor, with establishing the town as a storytelling center. And of course, she and her husband were among the original investors in Jonesborough's future. The Cherry Tree was the first craft shop that opened in Jonesborough.

Some say the bustle of historical restoration shook the dust off Jonesborough's ghosts and chased them out of the closet. Nearly everyone who has overhauled an historic house in Jonesborough has a ghostly tale to tell. When hammers began hammering, saws began sawing, and plaster dust drifted lazily through hallways, protesting denizens from the netherworld began to bang around creaking dwellings like angry children pitching hissy fits.

One woman in town was particularly unnerved at the shenanigans

Contents

going on in her historic dwelling. The walls shook at night with ghostly pounding. Objects moved around the house without explanation. She even heard someone talking in the hallway when she knew she was the only person in the house. The disturbances got so bad that the woman seriously considered selling her 150-year-old home. Her jangled nerves couldn't take it any longer.

After a particularly noisy (not to mention sleepless) night, the woman had finally had enough. With both feet firmly planted on her freshly sanded wide-planked floors, she stood at the top of the stairs and shouted down the darkened stairwell to whatever might be listening.

"I don't know who you are, but you are driving me crazy. You needn't worry about your house. I'm just trying to put it back the way it was when it was built.

"I'll make a deal with you," she continued. "If you stop making all that racket, I'll make the house better than it was when you lived in it."

After that the house was quiet. Lesson learned: A reassured poltergeist is often a quiet poltergeist.

Like every restored old town, Jonesborough is rife with ghostly tales. Historical events tend to produce ghosts like a bureaucracy produces headaches.

Jonesborough is an historic town in more ways than one. The vicinity around Jonesborough was the home of Tennessee icon John Sevier, the first governor of Tennessee. Andrew Jackson began his law career in the town in 1788.

Furthermore, Jonesborough is the oldest town in Tennessee. In 1779, the North Carolina General Assembly passed legislation to provide the first permanent settlement in the newly formed Washington District of western North Carolina. (There was, of course, no state of Tennessee until June 1, 1796, when President George Washington signed the bill.) The settlement was to be named Jonesborough in honor of the North Carolina patriot, the Honorable Willie (pronounced "Wiley") Jones.

In 1780, Jonesborough was surveyed and laid out by John Gilliland, who was paid $1,115 for the work. Settlers began moving in, and the town flourished.

In the first years of its existence, Jonesborough was an important town. It was the commercial and political gateway to the west. Jonesborough was a center of trade, and it was a jumping-off place for settlers crossing the Allegheny Mountains, heading west.

On August 23, 1784, delegates from Washington, Sullivan, and Greene Counties met in Jonesborough to plan the proposed new State of

Franklin. Western settlers had been neglected by the State of North Carolina. For one thing the state refused to move on marauding Indians, a problem that was plaguing settlers. North Carolina even refused to recognize treaties or business dealings that settlers made with the Indians. But the state, on the other hand, insisted that inhabitants still be levied for the full amount of their share of taxes. Understandably, western settlers felt they were getting no return on their investment.

In the meantime Shawnee and Cherokee Indians continued to raid settlements up and down the frontier; and settlers, trying to defend themselves without help from a well-armed militia, were killed by the dozens. Entreaties for help to the North Carolina legislature were ignored.

The North Carolinians decided to secede. They applied to the U.S. Congress for statehood. Statehood insured that Federal troops would be sent in to help fight Indians.

Six months later a second convention was held to adopt a new constitution. And in 1785, a general assembly chose John Sevier as governor of the proposed new State of Franklin.

Colonel John Tipton, who owned a farm near Jonesborough, was a North Carolina loyalist and, as such, was a political foe of Sevier. One day while Sevier was out of town fighting Indians, Tipton and his cohorts chased the Franklin magistrates out of the courthouse in Jonesborough. A bench warrant was issued for Sevier's arrest.

Sevier was duly captured, but he later escaped. No matter, though. The die was cast. The new government rapidly fell apart, and by 1788 the "Lost State of Franklin" was just a memory.

In the spring of 1788, 21-year-old Andrew Jackson arrived in Jonesborough from Morganton, North Carolina, riding one horse and leading another. The horse he rode on was a race horse. He was also well armed, packing a set of twin pistols and a shotgun. Accompanying Jackson's arrival in Jonesborough was a rambunctious pack of foxhounds.

On May 12, 1788, Jackson produced credentials certifying his right to read the law in North Carolina. While rooming with Christopher Taylor, whose two-story log house was located about a mile outside town, Jackson practiced law in Jonesborough in a one-room log courthouse. A little more than a year later, he left for greener pastures in Nashville.

Throughout the years, Jonesborough continued to grow, increasing in importance as more and more settlers crossed the rugged Alleghenies, settling in on farms along the fertile valleys of the Nolichucky and Holston Rivers, and along the banks of Little Limestone Creek.

Jonesborough, as I said, was a center of politics and commerce. In

1858 the first railroad engine steamed into town. More houses were built. More businesses opened.

The town survived the ravages of overflowing rivers, raging blizzards, a devastating cholera epidemic in 1873, and numerous fires—not to mention the War Between The States. But Jonesborough couldn't overcome progress.

For some reason Jonesborough failed to increase substantially in size or in population. Major railroads passed it by. No industry of any size developed. The town remained a sleepy farming community, while Johnny-come-lately Johnson City, 10 miles to the east, became a full-fledged city. In the 1960s, when Johnson City was expanding along North Roan Street, business in Jonesborough fell off to nearly nothing.

Then Jonesborough rediscovered its important role in the history of East Tennessee. Once that was recognized, townspeople got to work, renovated buildings, opened shops, and began an active campaign to attract tourists to town.

The ghosts of Jonesborough, like the town's remarkable history, were there all along. Now it was high time for them, like Jonesborough itself, to come out of the closet.

What are these scary things we call ghosts? Where did they come from? And why do they behave like they do?

In trying to explain ghosts, we are forced to deal with so-called ghost logic. Hauntings tend to follow predictable scenarios, and ghosts (at least, the ghosts in folklore) seem to follow established—even rigid— patterns of behavior. For instance, ghosts appear to repeat the same action over and over again, usually in the same location. Thus the tormented English ghost of Catherine Howard, the unfortunate wife of Henry VIII, forever runs through the halls of Hampton Court "with 'er 'ead tucked underneath 'er arm."

And at the Christopher Taylor cabin in Jonesborough, the shade of Andrew Jackson is always seen pausing at the door where it looks around before entering. It's like playing a video tape, over and over again in an endless loop.

A ghost can be defined as the lingering spirit of something—person or animal—that is dead. There are also reports of ghosts of inanimate objects like trains and ships, but these are quite rare.

A ghost is either visible (an apparition) or makes itself known through noises and the moving of objects (a poltergeist). Sometimes the ghost is neither seen nor heard, but a person may feel that it is there just the same (a presence).

There is some question as to whether a ghost has a mind of its own. Can it reason or even think independently? Or is the sight of a ghost really, as many experts think, part of a psychic "movie" of a past event, played over and over again?

Have you ever walked into a room and felt something unseen was there with you, lurking in the shadows? Have you ever sat in the living room watching television and heard footsteps overhead—and you knew no one was on the second floor? Remember how scared you might have been when confronted by the unknown?

People tend to be afraid of ghosts. But then, people tend of be afraid of anything they don't completely understand. Scientists have worked to help us understand the supernatural. Over the years they have espoused a number of theories about where ghosts come from and why they exist:

A ghost is the spirit of a person who has died but is unaware he is dead. Therefore it tries to go about its earthly business as if nothing has happened.

A ghost is the spirit of a person who may have died before completing some sort of worldly business. Therefore, it returns, trying to tie up loose ends of its life.

A ghost may return to identify the person who murdered him.

A ghost may appear to a living person to point out the location of something valuable—a deed or buried treasure.

A ghost may appear to the living to reassure them. There are hundreds of stories about deceased parents appearing to their children in moments of great personal crisis.

Whether or not you believe in ghosts, witches, or demons is unimportant. In this book, I have tried to provide a balance of all the different types of stories that float around Jonesborough—both those that are alleged to be actual encounters with ghosts as well as those which are plainly figments of someone's imagination.

These stories are part of our folklore. They have been handed down orally from person to person over the years. The first written version of many of these stories is contained in this book.

Jonesborough and Washington County, as can easily be seen, are rich in folklore and tradition. Early settlers consisted of a rich ethnic mix of cultures—Scot-Irish, English, Welsh, Irish, German, Scandinavian, and French Huguenots. Each brought the folklore of his native land to the New World. Here it mixed with the folklore of other cultures—including that of Native Americans. The result is that particular brand of tale that we call Southern Appalachian folklore.

The following is a newspaper account of the ghostly activity in Jonesborough's most infamous haunted house. The house belonged to Brigadier General Alfred E. "Mudwall" Jackson of the Confederate Army, commander of troops in upper East Tennessee. (He was nicknamed "Mudwall" to distinguish him from the more famous "Stonewall" Jackson of Virginia.) The house was also used as a makeshift hospital during the War Between The States. Afterward, Jackson rented the house to a number of tenants. The brick structure was torn down around the turn of the century.

The following article from the Jonesborough *Herald and Tribune* (April 1, 1875) has been reparagraphed and partially repunctuated for easier reading.

Haunted House: Jonesborough
People Excited

It has been reported for a number of years by different families who have resided in the "Jackson House," situated south of the railroad and near the corporation of Jonesborough, that the house was haunted.

Our citizens gave the report but little attention as they believe it was imaginary and not real with those who made the report.

It may be proper to state that it is a large brick house with many rooms. It is located on a beautiful hill and surrounded by trees and shrubbery.

In that house now lives Mr. Nathan Morrell and family, who are well-known to many of our citizens. They are honest [and] hard-working with a respectable family. They have never, until recently, believed in haunts or hobgoblins. In fact, they say they were taught by their parents, when children, not to believe any such reports, as it was all imaginary and not real.

Being anxious to know the particulars of what might be seen and heard at the house, we inquired of Mr. Morrell as to the truth of the report that is being circulated in regard to the mysterious knockings, walking, crying, and groaning. He said he was going to stop talking about the mystery, especially to those who had the audacity to doubt the truthfulness of what he said in regard to it.

We assured him that we had the utmost confidence in him as a truthful and honest gentleman, and desired him to state to us all he knew about it.

After having assured him of our earnestness and confidence in him, he proceeded to say that often at night they could hear the strange and mysterious noise in one of the rooms upstairs which sounded like a man walking with a cane, and they could hear him coming down and going up the stair steps, and that he would, after many a time, pound upon the door and turn the knob of the lock as though he was trying to enter the room the family occupies.

At other times, they could hear groaning and crying which sounded like a woman in distress.

They have often tried to find the cause for these mysterious doings but, as yet, have never been able to see anything that would give them light or information.

Mr. Elbert Morrell, who resides in the country, visited his father last Monday [March 29], at which time he heard a very strange noise that appeared to be in the wall of the house. He was also alarmed by his chair, in which he was sitting, raising up suddenly several inches, accompanied by a loud report as though it had been struck by a plank or board.

Many persons still doubt the correctness of these reports, while there are others who believe them and would not be willing to join a company to watch for and, if possible, catch the "bugaboo."

Should any new developments take place in the future, we will take pleasure in publishing them for the benefit of our readers.

The Murderous Tree

One of these days I'm going to write a book containing nothing but the best of the hundreds of "lovers' lane" tales I've collected in upper East Tennessee over the years. "Lovers' lane" yarns, as I like to call them, are the most common type of story told by people who are not professional storytellers.

These are stories meant to be told spontaneously in lonely places where the sun seldom shines, in tangled laurel thickets in the middle of the night, in the backseat of automobiles, around blazing camp-fires, or in the relative safety of one's own house.

These are tales of pure horror, featuring impossible beasts, horrible monsters, and mad killers. You probably remember a few of them from your youth—you've probably even told a few of them yourself. These are stories, for example, that generations of young men have told their female companions while parked in lonely, secluded spots in the country.

One of the most famous of these "lovers' lane" tales is the story of a deranged killer who stalks the woods looking for unsuspecting victims. He has only one hand. In place of the other hand is a murderous hook with which he unmercifully slashes his victims.

There are many other tales like this one—usually featuring a revenge motif. I heard the following story from a teenage friend of mine in Jonesborough and thought I would include it in this anthology. It is one of my favorites of the genre.

Ol' Mose was one of the first white men to set foot on the west slope of the Unaka Mountains in Northeast Tennessee. He settled there even before Jonesborough was built. For 30 years, Ol' Mose hunted and trapped from the Holston River to the French Broad River—hardly ever seeing another white man except for an occasional long hunter that passed through his territory.

He made fast friends with the Cherokee and was able to live in peace with his Indian neighbors. He numbered among his Indian friends Attakullakulla and Old Tassel. In fact, it was Old Tassel, the famous Cherokee chief, who gave Ol' Mose his Indian name—"Man Who Lives in a Tree."

Mose was a tiny man. There was plenty of room for him to move around in the bowels of the hollow oak. He could even stretch out to his full length on a mattress of leaves if he wanted to sleep inside. But he spent most of his nights sleeping under the stars where he was most content.

The hole in the tree trunk which served as a doorway was just large enough for him to squeeze through but small enough to keep out larger, dangerous animals that lived in the surrounding forest. Unfortunately, the hole failed to keep out the most dangerous enemy of all—man.

If Mose had been killed by a bear or a wildcat, that would have been one thing. Long hunters were often killed by wild animals that were hungry or protecting their territory from intruders.

But humans were supposed to be different—they knew better than to kill another human being. That was a crime that cried out for vengeance. So when Ol' Mose died violently one night at the hands of another long hunter, the Indians said it was his vengeful spirit that became part of the tree.

There was good reason to believe Ol' Mose had been murdered by a rival trapper. A stranger—a long hunter no one had seen in those parts before—had been spotted nearby in the woods. One day, the stranger disappeared and was never seen again. Then Mose was discovered murdered. Soon after that, Mose's tree mysteriously disappeared—as if it had been wiped from the face of the earth. The Indians claimed Mose's spirit had infested the tree and had made it come alive.

Folks say the tree still walks the forest—seeking revenge for the murdered, tormented soul that inhabits it. On moonlit nights it stalks, slowly pulling itself along the forest floor, its roots acting like horrible legs.

The tree makes no noise whatever as it moves about. Its intended victim is unaware of the tree's presence until it is too late. By then the screaming victim is entwined in the horrible limbs, pulled toward the gaping hole in the trunk until, at last, the body disappears forever.

One night several years ago, a romantic couple had parked on a remote dirt road somewhere near Jonesborough. It was midsummer, but the weather was cool—not hot and muggy. Crickets chirped in the river bottom. Occasional clouds drifted across a yellow, full moon.

Since the boy's uncle owned the farm on which they were parked, there was no chance the couple would be surprised by the police. All in all, it was the perfect setting—and night—for a little serious necking.

The couple settled in for an evening of togetherness. A half hour later, someone could have set off a stick of dynamite next to the car and it wouldn't have disturbed the lovers inside. They were so occupied, in fact, they failed to notice a dark shadow lurking in a nearby grove.

The shadow slowly approached and finally stood beside the automobile. Like tentacles, its limbs reached out for the well-fogged windows. Then with a mighty thrust, the wooden tendrils smashed through the glass and wrapped themselves around the throat of the young man. His surprised, horrified companion screamed for all she was worth.

Coughing and gasping for air, the boy felt himself being pulled through the shattered window.

His terror-stricken girlfriend screamed again and pushed against the opposite door. She turned and tried to open it. The door was jammed tight.

"Help me!" the boy gasped. Then he felt the horrible tendrils tighten around his fleshy neck. His cut and bleeding body was already pulled halfway through the window, his legs kicking wildly.

Finally he was outside on the ground. He struggled to his feet, his hands grasping at his throat, trying to wiggle free.

For the first time, the girl clearly saw the attacker. It was a tree! A horrible, living tree. She screamed again, and the sound of her terror echoed through the hills. But the nearest house was a mile away and no one heard.

Suddenly the back door of the car flew open and she tumbled to the ground. When she stood up, she saw the tree standing over the limp body of her boyfriend. Slowly the limbs coiled around the body and drew it into a hole in the side of the trunk, where it disappeared.

Then the tree was moving again. This time it was coming toward her!

The girl screamed, turned, and fled into the woods, the murderous tree on her heels. She crashed through the thick vines, her hair tangling in the undergrowth when she fell. She sat still and listened. She could no longer hear her pursuer. But instinctively she knew it was there—lurking somewhere in the woods.

With some difficulty, the girl untangled her hair, sprang to her feet, and continued running. A cloud drifted in front of the moon. Now she could see no more than a few feet in front of her.

Once again she fell. But this time her long hair was hopelessly tangled in vines. She tried to get up but was held fast.

She heard something in front of her and she looked up. A giant, shadowy form loomed over her. She screamed and jerked her head, trying to get loose. It was hopeless.

Giant limbs reached out for her. She felt them entwine around her neck, and she tried to scream again. But the cry was choked out before it even began. And soon there was no breath left in her.

Only an encroaching darkness....

For two centuries the murderous tree, containing Ol' Mose's angry spirit, has searched for victims—seeking revenge. It haunts lonely lovers' lanes because the pickings are so easy there. The lovers are so preoccupied that they do not notice the horror lurking just outside their fogged-up windows—that is, until it is too late to escape with their lives.

Perhaps *your* favorite spot will be the site of the next attack. If it is, *then Heaven help you*!

As I said in the introduction to this book, nearly every historic house in Jonesborough boasts at least one resident spook, but the scenario of each haunting is essentially the same. Most hauntings first become apparent when renovations begin on the individual houses. The tales have a sameness about them. I think when you hear one story about a restless spirit kicking up its heels in a freshly renovated house, you've heard them all.

Invariably the ghost starts acting up when construction begins, and the harassed resident of the house is forced to seek peace with the spirit by promising that the house will not be irrevocably harmed by the ongoing renovations.

The following, however, is a familiar-sounding ghost story with a big difference....

The Ghost Who Hated the Confederacy

The previous resident of Gerald and Sue Henley's historic home on Main Street in Jonesborough lived there for 92 years. Although she was not born in the house, Miss Martha had come to Jonesborough with her parents at the age of two. When the Henleys bought the property, they discovered that Miss Martha had left a treasure trove of aging photographs, including one of herself as a baby, playing happily in the house's sunny backyard around the turn of the century.

Sue Henley said Miss Martha never threw anything away. "That was wonderful for us. She left a lot of wonderful old pictures and things like that in the house. We had wonderful collections that we gave to the

Jonesborough/Washington County Regional Museum."

The house on Main Street was built in the 1840s by Jonesborough tailor Jacob Naff. For a time in the 1850s, he operated a tailor shop in one of the rooms. Naff sold the house in 1863 at the height of the War Between The States.

The only private residence presently in the central business district, the Henley house is of a saddlebag design with a stairway going up the center and a parlor on either side. The house is small as far as older homes in Jonesborough go. The rooms average only 16 by 20 feet, with 10-12 foot ceilings. Sue describes the house as "comfortable."

Entering the house was like walking into a time machine. "The house is almost all original," Sue told me. "The floors were still original when we bought it. The windows were all original, as were the ceilings and fireplaces. No one had ever gone in and changed that house."

But there were still renovations to be made. Time has the potential to ravage even the most sturdily built house. And this one had had almost no improvements or updating for nearly a century.

"We had to totally reroof, rewire and replumb everything," Sue told me. "We had to strip off every inch of wallpaper. It took us three and a half years to do everything that we needed to do to that house."

With the status quo in check for 92 years, it stood to reason, therefore, that the ghost living in the Henley home might protest changes the new residents were making, as well as their noisy, dusty activities.

The trouble with the ghost started the first night. On the outside of the bedroom door was a hook and eye latch—the kind found on an old-fashioned screen door. In order to use the lock, the hook had to be turned all the way around so that it would fit through the eye.

"We got up the morning after we had moved into the house," Sue said, "and tried to get out of the bedroom. The door wouldn't open. We were locked in—it was latched."

After that, Sue said she and her husband, Gerald, tried a hundred times to get the hook to latch by itself—but, of course, it wouldn't.

Other strange and unexplained things happened in the house during renovations.

"The week we moved into the house," Sue said, "Gerald had gone out to eat and I was alone. There was a huge stepladder standing out in the foyer that Gerald was using to paint. I was downstairs in the den.

"The door to the den opens directly into the foyer. About nine or ten at night I heard the front door open and I thought that Gerald had come home. He didn't come into the den to say hello. Three or four minutes went by—still no Gerald. Then I heard this ladder move across the wood floor. It was a huge ladder, heavy. I could hardly move it by myself.

Well, that's strange, I thought to myself. *He's started to paint again and hasn't even stopped in to say hello.*

"So I went out into the foyer, but no one was there. In fact, there was still no one in the house but me! And it scared the holy heck out of me!"

Although strange things have happened throughout the house, the center of the haunting seems to be located in the east bedroom where the Henleys had their encounter with the lock the first night. For the first year they lived in the house, they were forced to live in that bedroom while the rest of the house was being worked on. So the ghost had ample opportunity to make itself known to them.

"Actually, I'm comfortable in the house and not afraid," Sue said. "But the one room that I do have strange feelings in is that east bedroom—the one that faces the ice cream parlor on Main Street."

Even Gerald has odd feelings in the room. One morning he was putting on his clothes. Suddenly, he felt a presence, like something was watching him. Then the hair stood straight up on the back of his neck.

"I have a friend in Kingsport," Sue said, "who says she can *sense* things about houses. She came to the house one night for a party we were giving, and went upstairs to look around. When she returned, she had the strangest look on her face. (I might add that I never had told her anything about our experiences in the house.)

" 'Did anything strange ever happen in that bedroom upstairs on the east side of the building?' she asked.

"And I said, 'Well.... We got locked in that bedroom the first night we slept in it.'

"Then she said, 'I know you're going to think I'm crazy, but I see things. Right beside your fireplace, there's a woman sitting in the corner. She is a young girl—like 18 or 20 years old. She is hunkered down with her hands around her knees. And she had been in that room for a long, long time.' "

In 1992 Sue Henley conducted one of her periodic guided tours of the house. One of the guests was a journalist from Memphis.

After the tour, Sue was talking to the other guests in the foyer. The journalist approached Sue and asked, "Does anything strange or unusual happen in that bedroom upstairs?"

Sue was startled. She had heard that same question before. "Well.... Why?"

The journalist was obviously not kidding when she replied, "Well, I know you're going to think I'm totally crazy, but I sense things. *There is* something in that room upstairs. I felt a presence. I felt something strange."

Sue told me the journalist said she had had experiences like that before. A friend of hers had just bought a house in Memphis, and the girl was very uncomfortable there. She called her journalist friend and asked her to visit.

"There was an arch in that house," the journalist told Sue. "And the minute I walked into that house, I knew whatever had happened there had happened under that arch.

"Well, they did research and found out that during the Civil War, people—I don't know who—had been *lynched under the arch of that house*."

The woman added that she had felt the same strangeness about the east bedroom in Sue Henley's house!

Although neither Sue nor Gerald Henley has seen an apparition in the house, Sue, especially, has witnessed some very odd activity. One week in the summer of 1992 was an especially active time for the ghost.

"Gerald's mother had given him a little coconut that was used as a string holder," Sue remembered. "Gerald had remembered it from his kitchen at home 40 years ago. I had the coconut hanging on a hook on the kitchen fireplace.

"My niece was standing in the kitchen, and I was on the back porch. All of a sudden, that coconut came flying right off the hook. It fell down on the hearth; and the eye, on which the string was hooked, broke off. There was no one even close to it.

"That happened on a Sunday. The next day we returned home to find something else had happened.

"We had a plate rack above the door in the kitchen. There are things sitting up there like crocks and metal pots and pans. When we came home, two pieces were sitting in the middle of the floor.

"Later that day, or maybe the next, I was standing at the sink and washing dishes. I've got a lot of open shelves in my kitchen, with hundreds of things sitting on them. One of these was a little cut glass, antique toothpick holder.

"As I said, I was washing dishes. All of a sudden that toothpick holder flew off the shelf, hit the middle of the floor, and shattered into a million pieces. There was no natural reason for it.

"Later on, when I had put dishes in the dishwasher, I opened the door of the dishwasher to let the steam out. Then I left the kitchen for a few seconds. When I returned, I discovered two of the dishes had flown out of the dishwasher and were lying in the middle of the kitchen floor. No one was around the dishwasher!

"All this happened within one week's time last summer. But since then, nothing else like that has happened."

In addition to its poltergeist activity, the ghost in the Henley house also appears to be a trickster—and maybe even a politically-minded trickster with a sly sense of humor.

"I have some antique jewelry," Sue said, "and one of my favorite pieces is a very inexpensive cameo. This incident occurred at the time of the first Civil War reenactment in Jonesborough.

"I thought I would wear the cameo to the Confederate ball. I was in a real hurry to get dressed, and when I went to look for the cameo it was gone. All my other jewelry was there, but the cameo was gone. I was heartsick, but I didn't have time to look for it any further that night.

"The next day and the following week, I took my entire bedroom apart looking for that cameo. I took all the blankets off the bed. I looked under the bed, under the rugs, and took everything out of the closet and the dresser drawers. The cameo was nowhere to be found.

"Six or eight weeks later I walked into the bedroom. It was the middle of the day. And lying out about 12 inches from the foot of the bed, right on the carpet in plain sight, the chain neatly folded, was the cameo. I instantly had cold chills all over my body! Maybe the ghost had taken the cameo but, at least, had brought it back."

"Why had the ghost taken the cameo in the first place?" I asked Sue.

"Well," she answered with a smile, "I figured this much out. The ghost knew I was going to a Confederate ball, and it was a Unionist. It was clearly speaking to me that it highly disapproved of where I was going."

Harbingers of Death

Banshees, like vampires and werewolves, are essentially products of Old World folklore. When our forebears first landed in America, stories of these and other monsters came across on the boat with them. The stories originated in England, Ireland, Scotland, France, Germany, and other countries in Europe.

The Irish legend of the banshee, a spirit whose wail foretells death, has existed for hundreds of years. Early Irish settlers brought the legend with them when they helped settle upper East Tennessee. In some cases, the story remained essentially the same as it had in their homeland. But, as in all folklore, variations on the "wail of death" theme evolved over the years, especially since the Irish were heavily influenced by the folklore of Germans and other ethnic groups.

There are some people in and around Jonesborough that, even today, still believe in the "wail of death," though they might not attribute it directly to the Irish banshee. Their superstitions, however, are variations on a familiar theme.

According to one local superstition, for example, if a dog is heard to wail before a dead person is buried, and the body is still in the house, a member of the immediate family will die within a year. Another superstition is that the hoot of an owl also foretells an imminent death in the family.

According to German tradition, the sins of the body escape the coffin just before burial in the form of a black dog. After the body is buried, the spectral dog remains near the family, and its howling warns of the impending death of a family member.

For most people, the possibility of foretelling the future—especially predicting one's own death or the death of a loved one—is particularly frightening. How many of us want to know the exact hour of our own demise? Some kinds of information are better left to the unknown. But occasionally this kind of unwelcome information is thrust upon us, whether we like it or not.

Take, for example, the experience of John C. John was handy with tools, a very useful skill in turn-of-the-century Jonesborough. In fact he could fix almost anything that was broken.

John C. was also superstitious, according to his granddaughter, Ellen. "Our family is of pure German descent," she told me as we sat in her well appointed home just inside the Jonesborough city limits. "His father was an immigrant, and my grandfather was born in this country—near Kingsport."

For a time John C. worked for the Clinchfield Railroad as a track layer. When the line was finally completed in 1909, he moved his family to Jonesborough. Since he was so good with his tools, he soon earned a reputation as a "Mr. Fixit" around town.

"My grandfather believed that the world was alive with spirits of the dead," Ellen said. "And his father believed just like him. Both were uneducated. And both earned a living with their hands.

"One of Papaw's strongest beliefs was that the howl of a black dog could foretell the death of a member of the family. He said such a dog followed our family wherever they went. Then when one of them was about to die, the dog would appear and howl mournfully. He called it a 'black dog of hell'."

The granddaughter, nearly 70 years old, sat up straight in her chair and looked at me sternly over her wire-rimmed glasses. "Are you superstitious?" she asked ominously.

"I do have my moments," I answered, thinking that she might be joking with me. "I don't like Friday the 13th very much. But I'm sure that's all very silly, and one of these days I might grow out of it."

She frowned. "Don't be too sure about that," she replied. "I've lived a great many years more than you, and I still get nervous about Friday the 13th. And I don't like spilled salt or broken mirrors either."

"What about the black dog?" I asked.

Ellen sat back in her chair and relaxed a little. "I believe in the black dog, and I believe he's here with us right now. Maybe in this room. But you can't see or hear him. Not until it's time for someone to die. Then he'll appear, just as sure as you're born."

I glanced around the room nervously. She noticed my apprehension, and the corners of her mouth curved in a little smile. Then she said, "Papaw had an experience with the black dog once when I was just a little girl. He had come home late one night after a hard day's work. His wife usually had supper ready for him as soon as he walked in the door, but this time there was no food on the table, and Mamaw was nowhere to be found. He called to her, but she didn't answer.

"Then Papaw went back outside. He was worried. Both of them were creatures of habit and would become very nervous if one or the other did something out of the ordinary. For Mamaw not to be there with Papaw's supper ready was *very out of the ordinary*, indeed.

"Papaw returned to the house," the granddaughter continued. "Perhaps, he thought, she had run down to the grocery store for something or other. She would be back in a few minutes.

"He went over to his chair beside the woodstove and sat down. He was very tired and soon began drifting off to sleep, but he was suddenly awakened by a noise in the corner of the room. He opened his eyes just in time to see an enormous back dog, sitting in the corner, staring at him. Then the dog opened his mouth and began to howl—long, low, and mournful. Papaw stood up to chase the dog out of the house when it suddenly disappeared.

"A few moments later, there was a pounding on the door. Papaw opened it and found the Washington County sheriff standing there.

" 'John,' he said, 'you'd better come with me.'

" 'What's wrong, sheriff?'

" 'There's been an accident,' the sheriff replied nervously. 'Your wife was killed by a car in front of the Methodist Church.'

"Papaw told me this story a few years after it had happened. Of course, I didn't believe it—that is, until I saw and heard the dog myself. Ten minutes later, Papaw dropped dead of a heart attack. Years afterwards, I saw and heard the black dog again, this time two days before the death of my husband."

"So, then, you believe the black dog really foretells a death in the family?" I asked.

"Absolutely," she answered. "There are a lot of things in this world that we can't explain. I think this is one of them."

When I got up to leave, she said, "I want to tell you this. I saw the dog again—last night."

"Where?" I asked.

"At the foot of my bed. I was nearly asleep, just like my grandfather, when I suddenly opened my eyes and saw it sitting there, staring at me. Then it began to howl."

I sat back down in the chair. "Who do you think he was howling for this time?" I asked.

The old woman leaned forward. "My husband and I were childless. My parents are both dead. I have no close relatives left. *The only one left is me.*"

Two days later Ellen passed away. According to her doctor, she died of a heart attack. But, somehow, I have my doubts whether it was really a heart attack that killed her.

She was convinced she had seen the infamous black dog and that its baying was foretelling her death just like it had predicted the death of her grandmother, grandfather, and husband. When I left her house that afternoon, there was terror in her eyes. It was unmistakable.

She knew she was going to die, and to this day I can only wonder whether that terrible knowledge had not, in fact, *scared her to death*!

The Hero Comes Home

The Smiths (name has been changed) were a close-knit and loving family. Although both parents wanted many children, the union yielded only one son, James.

James was a big, strapping six-footer. He was also very intelligent and had graduated at the head of his class at a local high school. He had plans to attend East Tennessee State College in Johnson City (now called East Tennessee State University) and become a math teacher.

At the end of his first term at ETSC came the Japanese sneak attack on Pearl Harbor, and America was embroiled in World War II. Duty called and, like thousands of other young men, James put his education on hold and joined the Navy.

Attached to aircraft carriers for most of the war, he toured the Pacific and was involved in numerous naval engagements. Two carriers on which he had served were sunk. But throughout the entire ordeal, he never got so much as a scratch.

James's mother received regular letters from her son—about three a week. His father, who worked in a local clothing store, never tired of bragging about the heroism of his son. As far as he was concerned, James was winning the entire war single-handedly.

For nearly four years World War II dragged on, but the end was in sight. Germany had already surrendered on May 7, 1945, and the allies concentrated their might against the Japanese in the Pacific. How much longer could the empire of the rising sun last?

The Japanese, desperate because of a lack of trained pilots, began throwing untrained teenagers against the allied fleet. These children flew what amounted to flying bombs. Barely able to urge an airplane into the air, they crashed their aircraft into ships where they found them.

The suicide, or kamikaze, missions taxed allied shipping. Thousands of young sailors were killed. But the Japanese seemed to have no end of their own young men, blindly willing to sacrifice everything for emperor and country.

But in spite of the crippling effect of kamikaze missions, Americans felt the war was winding down to an end. Even the newspapers said so. There was an undercurrent of optimism in the country.

Mr. and Mrs. Smith were especially glad the war was being quickly won in the Pacific, because they would soon see their son again. They had not seen him since he came home on leave in 1944.

One day Mrs. Smith was working in her kitchen when she looked out of the window in time to see James walking across the lawn, his duffel bag slung over his shoulder. Her first thought was, "Why is he home? The war isn't even over yet."

But she yelped in delight and literally flew out the back door, into the yard. When he saw her coming, James smiled broadly, threw down his duffel bag and opened his arms wide to embrace his mother.

Just as Mrs. Smith reached James, she felt a cold chill, and her body passed through that of her son. Startled, she looked everywhere for him, but he had disappeared.

When she told her husband about the incident, Mr. Smith said that it must have been her imagination playing tricks. It must have been someone else that she mistook for her son.

A week later, the dreaded telegram arrived from the War Department. Her son was dead, killed when a kamikaze slammed into the U.S.S. Franklin, a carrier anchored just off Okinawa in the Pacific—the very hour that his mother had seen him in the yard.

One week later a memorial service for James Smith was held in a Jonesborough church. But James was not there—his body had been buried at sea.

Of course, the parents were grief-stricken at the death of their only son. And the incident in the Smiths' backyard was never mentioned again—that is, until Mrs. Smith told it to me a few years ago. She said her husband, an immensely practical man, never believed she had seen James in the yard.

But his mother said she was, nonetheless, oddly comforted. She knew that she had been allowed to see her son one last time.

Sometimes inanimate objects can take on ghostly characteristics. The following story illustrates a case in point.

The Dolls House

There are a lot of ghosts in Jonesborough. Perhaps that's because the town is so old. In fact, Jonesborough is the oldest town in Tennessee.

One historic house—a white board-and-batten structure on Main Street, just a block or two from the antique shops—belongs to Mrs. L. Because of the nature of Mrs. L's co-inhabitants, the home has been nicknamed "the dolls house" by Jonesborough residents.

Mrs. L. collects dolls—all kinds of dolls. Most of the dolls are very old. Many of them are bona fide antiques and are quite valuable.

Dolls sit on every shelf, table, and chair in the house. Glass eyes peer at the visitor from every nook and cranny. It's like dozens of people are watching you at the same time. The total effect is frightening.

It's scary enough when the dolls can be seen in broad daylight. But when the house is dark, it gets even scarier!

One day a local food market was asked to deliver a large sack of dog food to "the dolls house."

Mrs. L. had planned to be gone all day. But she dropped off her front door key by the store before she left. The delivery man could let himself in.

By the time the delivery man arrived at "the dolls house," it was late—nearly dark. And it was just beginning to rain.

The delivery man had been inside the house before. He thought it would be easy to find his way to the kitchen. Then, for some reason, he lost his way and was unable to find the light switch.

He felt his way through the hall, the heavy sack of dog food slung over his shoulder. Then his blood ran cold. Shivers went up and down his spine. He had the eerie feeling that someone was peering at him through the gloom. What really frightened him the most was he knew no one else was in the house!

Finally after much fumbling around, he found the light switch and clicked it on. There in the corner stood a three-foot-tall "Baby Jane" doll, its eyes *staring directly at him.*

Dolls are not the only occupants of Mrs. L's house. She said ghosts live there, too.

Mrs. L. said she was sitting on a couch in her living room watching television one night. To her right was a rocking chair. All was quiet in the house because it was so late. Suddenly she saw a man dressed in old-fashioned clothes appear in the chair.

Mrs. L. knew right away that he was a ghost because she could see right through the figure. And she had seen him before.

She started to speak, but the ghost vanished before she could say a word.

When she goes out of town, Mrs. L. says she leaves the house in the care of several "watch ghosts." These ghosts, she says, take an active interest in the welfare of her home. Indeed, town residents report strange noises and flickering lights in the windows when the house is empty. Voices are clearly heard from within.

When Mrs. L. returns, the lights and ghostly noises stop.

I asked Mrs. L. whether her house was *really* in the care of "watch ghosts" when she was away. She smiled and answered, "Well, I'm not saying if it's really true or not. *But the idea that it is* sure helps keep burglars away!

Ever since Washington Irving wrote "The Legend of Sleepy Hollow," stories of headless apparitions have become quite popular in America. But tales of headless ghosts, especially the unfortunate ones searching for their lost noggins, have permeated Old World folklore for countless centuries.

The following tale was told to me by a 73-year-old Washington County woman who, in turn, had heard it from her father, a German who immigrated to America just after the turn of the century.

Amos and the Headless Ghost

Myron Strauss got an unexpected bonus when he and his family moved into the big white farmhouse in Washington County near Jonesborough. The house was at least a century old, and some of the local residents believed it was haunted. Mr. Strauss, however, was a no-nonsense person who didn't believe in ghosts—at least, that's what he loudly claimed to anyone who would listen.

Shortly after the family moved in, strange things began to happen in the house. Doors opened and closed by themselves. Noises were heard on the second floor. It sounded like a man walking—slowly hobbling along on an artificial leg. When the house was searched, no one was there.

According to local legend about the house, a one-legged Civil War veteran was murdered by a man who had come late one night to collect a gambling debt.

Awakened from a sound sleep, the old veteran was not in the best of moods to begin with. But when he was confronted by an angry man demanding money, the visit quickly turned ugly. There was a violent argument between the two men.

The veteran reached for his pistol; but before he could fire, the other man had lobbed off his head with an axe. Since that night, the ghost of the veteran is said to walk the house, looking for his severed head.

When the footsteps were first heard, Mr. Strauss said to his family, "We must have a ghost." He didn't take the noises seriously, though. But his nine-year-old son, Amos, did. The strange noises in the house frightened Amos, although he tried not to show it.

For months, the noises continued. Up until that time none of the family, nor any visitors, had seen a thing. But then, all that changed.

One night Amos Strauss was in bed. The room was almost dark. Only a dim, yellow light from a full moon shone through his bedroom window on the second floor. A summer breeze ruffled the curtains hanging on the open window. The house was quiet. It was the first night in weeks that the mysterious footsteps had not been heard.

Amos was nearly asleep when he heard someone call his name.

"Amos...."

Amos opened his eyes, expecting to see his father. Instead, he saw a black shadow standing next to his bed. It looked like a man—tall and wearing old-fashioned clothing. Amos's blood ran cold when he realized the figure did not have a head! It was the ghost!

"Amos!" the voice called again. Amos shuddered and pulled the covers up over his head.

"Amos. I won't hurt you. I need your help."

Slowly Amos pulled the covers away from his face. The ghost was still there. He sat up in bed.

"The basement, Amos," the ghost said. The voice sounded very far away. "Come to the cellar underneath the house, Amos. Help me to find my head."

Then the ghost vanished into the darkness. Amos looked around the room. He was alone.

Amos felt a strange urge that pulled him toward the basement. Slowly, he crawled out of bed and slipped on his britches and his shoes.

He walked down the stairs, through the first floor of the house, stopping at the basement door.

Amos was scared. He really didn't want to go any farther. But the strange feeling pulled him on. He had to open the door. That scared him even more. *He knew that the ghost of the headless man was waiting for him in the cellar.*

Slowly, Amos made his way down the rickety wooden stairs into the basement. It was quite dark, and he had to watch carefully so he would not trip and fall.

When he reached the dirt floor of the cellar, he looked around. A green glow came from one corner. As if by an unseen hand, Amos was pulled toward it.

Then Amos heard the voice again. "Pick up the shovel and dig," it said. "Dig there, right where you're standing."

After several minutes of shoveling, Amos's spade clanked against something hard and white. As he cleared the dirt away, the object began to take shape. Amos's eyes widened when he realized what he was doing.

He was digging up a human skull!

"Now step back," the voice said. Amos didn't have to be told twice. The black figure glided over the skull in the hole. A few seconds later, it turned to Amos. For the first time, Amos could see the ghost's face— smiling and very pleased with itself.

"Thank you, Amos," the ghost said gratefully. Then it vanished.

And ever since that night, the house has been quiet.

The Red-Haired Ghost

The little town of Jonesborough attracts craftspeople like deep holes in the river attract fish. There's no way of telling how many artists actually live in town. But everywhere one looks, skilled hands are busy making something.

Maybe the same thing applies to ghosts and their obvious attraction to Jonesborough. The people of Jonesborough are friendly toward ghosts. They seem to add to the atmosphere of the town. And nearly every building in town swarms with them—especially those ancient buildings located on Main Street.

No one, however, has been able to explain the spectral attraction to Jonesborough with any certainty. There's no explaining "ghost logic"— i.e., why do ghosts haunt certain locations, and ignore others.

Perhaps it's the age—or the agelessness—of the town that attracts ghosts. Historical places, as a rule, attract more shadows of the past than locations of more recent origin. That includes the main street, itself!

Jonesborough's history certainly boasts more than its share of momentous events, as well as a multitude of colorful, historical characters. This atmosphere provides an effective breeding ground for supernatural tales. And, as I said, there are plenty of tales knocking around Jonesborough.

In an earlier book of ghost tales, **Haints, Witches and Boogers** (John F. Blair, 1992), I related eyewitness accounts of how the shade of Andrew Jackson is often seen strolling down Main Street, headed in the general direction of the old log courthouse. Jackson, of course, was no stranger to Jonesborough, first appearing as a young lawyer in the spring of 1788, then later returning as a judge. Jackson practiced law of one sort or the other, off and on, in the town for almost 15 years.

I also explained that Jackson's ghost, dressed in period clothing with a tall beaver hat perched on his head, is seen by people walking on the opposite side but not by people on the same side of the street. The ghost frequently passes mere inches from the unaware pedestrians—or even through them!

Jackson's ghost is not limited to any particular building or spot in Jonesborough. In fact, his shade apparently ranges over the entire town—from the Christopher Taylor Cabin in the town park to the garden at Febuary Hill, home of the late Burgin Dossett, former East Tennessee State University president. And Jackson's ghost is not the only Jonesborough spook to behave in such a manner.

Like I said, Jonesborough attracts lots of craftspeople, as well as denizens from the ether. Here is a story told to me a few years ago by Carolyn Moore:

An itinerant carpenter arrived in town one day. As usual, he was warmly greeted by artisans and other craftspeople. They welcomed him so warmly and so well, in fact, that the carpenter fell in love with the town and decided to hang around for a while.

John (not his real name) secured quarters on the second floor of the building where Jonesborough Designer Craftsmen is now located. A long, wooden stairway led to his new apartment.

Each night when he quit work, John sat on his steps. He enjoyed the cool breezes of the evening and chatting with his new friends. One night John was visited by a strikingly beautiful red-haired girl. Of course, John was instantly attracted to her.

After a few minutes of pleasant conversation, the girl excused herself and left. Unfortunately John forgot to ask her name, so he had no idea who she was. But he was determined to find out. He wanted to see her again.

The next day, the first person John met on the street was Paul Fink, Jonesborough's historian until his death in 1980. The elderly Fink knew just about everyone in town, so John assumed he would recognize the girl if he described her. This he did with relish.

When John finished his description, the smile suddenly vanished from Fink's face.

"Yes," Fink told John. "I know who she was. Her name was Clara. Ten years ago she drowned in the Nolichucky River!"

The following is a "Jack Tale" from the Jonesborough/Washington County area that I really like, so I thought I would include it in this collection. There are hundreds (even thousands) of these fairy-tale-type stories in existence. The hero of most of the tales is a boy (or as in this case, a young man) named Jack who sets off from home to seek his fortune, has exciting adventures, and learns some important lessons in life along the way. Like most "Jack Tales," this one has a strong supernatural element.

Jack and the Evil Spirit

There was once a young man named Jack who lived with his widowed mother in a little cabin on the banks of the Nolichucky River. Jack's father, a wood carver, had died many years before. Since Jack's mother was old and could do little work, they were now very poor. Jack's fondest wish was to make enough money so his mother would never want for anything again. So one day, he decided to leave home and seek his fortune. Early one morning he kissed his mother goodbye and set out on his journey, carrying only one roll and a change of clothes in his pack.

For two days he traveled south along the banks of the winding Nolichucky River. On the third day he came upon a little cabin in the woods. He was very hungry by this time because he had eaten his roll on the second day. He was so hungry, in fact, that he decided to rap on the door and ask whoever answered it for a bite to eat.

The door opened a crack and an old woman peeped out—a woman who looked even older than Jack's mother.

"What d'ya want, young sir?" the old woman asked, wearing a lop-sided grin.

"Something to eat, ma'am," Jack answered. "I'm on a journey to seek my fortune, and I have had nothing to eat for a whole day."

The old woman laughed. "So it's food that you want, is it? Well, I think we can fix that. Then the old woman opened the door all the way and beckoned to Jack with a long, bony finger. "Come on in, young sir Come in."

Jack paused for a moment. Something was odd about the old woman and her cabin. She looked for all the world like a witch. Jack's mother had told him about such people, living alone in the depths of the forest. Witches were magic and, when riled, could be very dangerous. But the hunger in Jack's belly gnawed at him. Through the open door he could see a big black pot hanging over the fireplace. Something smelled good.

"Well, are you coming in?" the old woman asked impatiently.

Jack stepped through the door. Inside, the cabin was warm, but every-thing was in disarray. Pots, pans, and broken crockery littered the floor. Clothes were strewn everywhere. Bottles of mysterious liquids lined rough wooden shelves, and bowls of strange herbs and roots sat on the only table in the single room.

In one corner a rangy black cat stretched after waking up from a nap. But in another corner, Jack was surprised to see a beautiful young girl who sat rocking in a chair. She looked totally out of place in the cabin.

"Meet my daughter, young sir. Her name is Clarissa." It went without saying that Jack was very much taken with the young girl's beauty. He nodded shyly. Clarissa smiled sweetly, but said nothing and remained seated.

The old woman moved to the fireplace and uncovered the big iron pot. Then she picked up a ladle from the hearth and turned to Jack. "This rabbit stew is my best dish, young sir, so you're in luck. And there's plenty so you can have all you want."

Jack licked his chops while the old woman ladled the pungent con-coction into a big wooden bowl. Then she cleared off a corner of the table and set the bowl down along with a long loaf of freshly baked bread.

"Eat your fill," she said.

Jack didn't have to be told twice. When he finished the first bowl, he was given a second.

After he ate, the old woman served him a hot cup of strong tea. "Drink all of this," she said. "It will bring back your strength."

The tea tasted bitter, but Jack drank all of it. Then he thanked the woman for her generosity. The old woman smiled her crooked smile and said, "It's not charity, you're looking for, young sir. No. I'm sure of that. You want to earn your keep."

"I have strong arms," Jack replied. "If you have a wood pile, I can split firewood for you."

The old woman sat down and leaned across the table. "No, young sir. Firewood I have plenty of. It's Clarissa I'm thinking of."

Jack glanced uneasily at the young girl still sitting in the rocking chair. So far she had not uttered a single word. She only watched Jack closely.

"My daughter cannot speak. She's mute," the woman said.

"I'm sorry," Jack replied.

Then the old woman turned toward her daughter. Clarissa smiled shyly. The woman turned back to Jack. "You can help her speak again, young sir," she said. "And that's the repayment I want from you for this good meal."

Jack hardly knew what to say. "I'm not a doctor, ma'am. I don't see how I...."

"It's not a doctor she needs," the old woman answered. "No doctor can help my Clarissa regain her tongue. But you.... You *can help* her. And for that, you will be handsomely rewarded."

Jack glanced at Clarissa. Slowly she got out of her chair and made her way to the table. She sat down beside Jack and took his hand. The old woman smiled.

"Clarissa likes you, young sir," the woman said. "And what's more, she trusts you."

Jack turned to the old woman. "You said a doctor could not help your daughter regain her voice. Why?"

"Many years ago, my daughter talked just like anyone else. Oh, did she talk. I thought she would never stop.

"Then when she was about six years old, she wandered into the woods alone. I had warned her to stay close to the cabin, but you know how children are."

Jack nodded his head.

"There's an evil spirit in those woods, young sir. And that creature put a spell on her which took my daughter's voice away. And that same spirit is the only one that can give her voice back to her."

"How?" Jack asked.

The old woman shook her head sadly. "Look around you. You have noticed the things on the shelves and tables. For years I've been studying witchcraft, hoping to find a spell to bring Clarissa's voice back. I've become quite good at mixing potions and things, and I've helped a lot of people—that is, everyone but my Clarissa. In trying to help her I've failed. The magic of the evil spirit is just too strong."

"That explains all these bottles and bowls."

"Yes, that's what I said. But I'm afraid all the spells in the world can't compare with a heart that's brave and true—like I take yours to be.

"Your only thought is for your mother and her welfare. That is why you are on this journey. That is why I think you can help my Clarissa when I have only failed. What I'm asking of you is to take a little time to help my daughter."

Jack looked at the young girl who still held his hand. Her eyes were clear and blue. Billows of flaxen hair fell around her shoulders. Her lips were full and red. She smiled a little. Jack could not resist her and turned to the old woman.

"Very well, I will try to help."

Suddenly the young girl threw her arms around Jack and hugged him for all she was worth. Jack was caught by surprise—and he liked it.

"What must I do?" he asked.

"From this river, travel east until you come to a tall rock cliff. At the bottom of the cliff, you will find a cave. The spirit lives in there."

"Then what?"

"You must fight him to the death."

"With what? I have no weapon."

"With your hands, young sir. You cannot take a weapon with you into that cave. Only your bare hands."

What had Jack gotten himself into? What if the evil spirit killed him, or even took his voice away? Then he could not earn his fortune, and his mother would die in poverty.

Still he had given his word to the old woman and her daughter. He must at least try.

"Tonight you will sleep," the old woman said as she rose from her chair. "Tomorrow, you and Clarissa will travel to the cave. And may God be with you."

The next morning, Jack rose early. The old woman fixed him and Clarissa a good breakfast of eggs, ham, and grits. Then she packed some corn bread and salt pork and stuffed the food into Jack's pack.

"The cave is only a day's journey from here," she said as they prepared to leave. "I feel that you must attack the spirit early in the morning. That's when he's most vulnerable. He stalks the woods all night, so he's tired when he gets back to his cave."

"Yes ma'am," Jack answered uneasily.

"Just remember," she added. "You may fight him only with your bare hands. Take no weapon. Not even a club."

For the whole day Jack and Clarissa traveled eastward. The path through the forest was well used for a long distance, but it soon petered out to nothing. Luckily Jack had a good sense of direction, so he found his way through the woods easily.

Clarissa kept up with Jack's progress. That was good. He feared she might lag behind.

It was growing dark when the pair came to the edge of the forest. Across a great meadow the cliff loomed over them, nearly stretching to the sky. At the base of it was the cave. And in that cave was a horrible spirit that Jack must fight until one of them was destroyed.

The old woman had said that the evil spirit roamed the woods at night, so they had to hide until morning. Jack found a hollow log a short distance from the edge of the woods that was big enough for Clarissa and him to crawl into. There they sat and ate their supper as night fell.

After dark Jack heard a strange howling, unlike any that he had ever heard before. He glanced at Clarissa, who was staring out of the hole in the log and into the darkness. She turned to him with fear in her eyes.

"Is that him?" Jack asked, his voice shaking in fear.

Clarissa, who could hear perfectly well, nodded. She had heard that sound before. It was the spirit that had taken away her voice. Now he roamed the forest, looking for more victims.

Although Clarissa fell asleep early, Jack was up most of the night listening to the strange howling. What if the spirit looked into the log and discovered them? What would he do?

The forest began to lighten and the sun prepared to peep over the edge of the world. Clarissa stirred and opened her eyes. She nudged Jack, who awoke with a start.

The morning was alive with the singing of birds, and the mists of dawn had barely cleared away when Jack and Clarissa reached the sheer face of the rock cliff. Almost immediately Jack found an opening in the side of the cliff.

"That must be the spirit's cave," he whispered to Clarissa, who nodded in agreement. Then he added, "You stay out here where you'll be safe."

The young girl shook her head "no."

Jack put a hand on her shoulder. "You must stay here, Clarissa. If something happens to me, then you must run with all your might back home."

But the girl stubbornly refused to budge. Finally Jack, in frustration, shrugged his shoulders and gave up trying to convince her to wait. She was bound and determined to go into the spirit's cave with him, and he doubted whether anything short of hog-tying the girl would stop her.

Inside the cave it was pitch dark. Jack could barely see anything. The floor of the cave was rocky and uncertain, and both he and Clarissa stumbled but didn't fall. Jack held tightly to Clarissa's hand.

Far back in the cave they heard a howl—a sound like the wind blowing. But Jack knew better. There was no wind, not even a breeze, in the cave. It was the sound of the evil spirit.

The sound got nearer until it sounded like it came from behind a huge boulder right in front of them. Jack was so close that he dared not utter a sound. Instead, he placed his hand on Clarissa's shoulder and motioned for her to stay put. Clarissa looked at him for a moment as if to protest, but she finally agreed. Then she leaned over and kissed Jack on the cheek.

No woman had kissed him before—except, of course, his mother—but there was no time for Jack to be embarrassed. Slowly he made his way to the boulder and peeked around it. He saw a figure—a shadow really—sitting on the edge of a large rock. It was bent over with its hands around its knees, as if resting. Suddenly it sat up and turned toward Jack. The figure had no face except two eyes—eyes that glowed yellow in the dark.

Jack boldly stepped from behind the boulder, in plain sight of the spirit. The creature stood up and lunged at Jack, picking him up as if he were a leaf and flinging him against a hard rock wall. All the breath left Jack's body from the impact. Then he slid down the smooth, rocky face. He looked up and saw the spirit standing over him. The spirit hissed and picked Jack up again, this time throwing him face down against the hard floor of the cave.

Jack rolled over, gasping for air. He slowly stood up. The spirit lunged again, but this time Jack stepped aside. The creature flew past Jack and hit the cave wall. It turned and hissed again. Jack assumed a fighting stance, his legs spread apart, his fists balled up.

The spirit lunged once again and Jack stepped aside just in time. The spirit missed again. He turned toward Jack, and his yellow eyes turned red in rage.

Jack's brain was moving in high gear. How could he defeat this creature? The spirit was obviously much stronger than he was. There were plenty of rocks on the floor of the cave that he could use as a weapon, but the old woman had warned him that he must use only his bare hands in fighting the spirit. What was he to do?

The spirit charged again in a rage. This time it grabbed Jack and flung him against the boulder behind which Clarissa was standing. Once again, Jack had the breath knocked out of him. His prospects for winning the fight looked dark. In fact, he thought there was no chance that he would win at all. He was clearly outmatched by this magical creature.

Then, suddenly, Clarissa stepped from behind the boulder, in plain view of the spirit. She stood there calmly. The evil spirit saw her and turned. Jack also saw what was happening and struggled over to where she was standing. The evil spirit hissed, but Clarissa didn't move.

"Get back!" Jack yelled. But the girl didn't move.

The spirit hissed again and began to charge the girl. There was only one thing for Jack to do. He bravely stood between Clarissa and the spirit, defying the evil creature to try to kill the girl.

Suddenly the spirit stopped in its tracks and stared at the young man. Then the creature let out a horrible scream that echoed throughout the cave. But Jack bravely stood his ground.

The evil spirit slowly started to disappear, the screaming growing fainter with every passing second.

Finally the spirit was gone, and Jack and Clarissa were alone in the cave. Jack stared into the darkness for a long moment, then sank to the cave's floor. He was kneeling there, trying to regain his breath, when he felt a gentle hand on his shoulder.

"He's gone," a soft, feminine voice said. "You've won, Jack. You've won."

Jack turned and saw that the voice belonged to Clarissa. He rose slowly.

"You can talk!" he exclaimed. "Your voice is back!"

Clarissa smiled her prettiest smile. "Yes, Jack. When you destroyed the evil spirit, his spell over me was broken."

But Jack looked uneasily around the cave. He still expected the spirit to be lurking somewhere in the darkness, waiting to lunge at him any second. "But how did I destroy the spirit? I never laid a hand on him!"

"Your goodness destroyed the spirit, Jack," Clarissa replied. "When you stepped in front of me, the spirit saw you were ready to sacrifice everything—even your life—to protect me. Your goodness destroyed his evil."

Jack looked puzzled. "Is that why you insisted on coming with me into the cave. Did you know exactly what was going to happen?"

"Not exactly, Jack," Clarissa answered in a clear, strong voice. "But I had a good idea what I must do. And it worked. The evil spirit has been destroyed, and my voice has returned. The spell is broken. And it's all because of you."

Then she kissed him again.

When Jack and Clarissa returned home, Clarissa's mother thanked Jack for helping her daughter. Then she went to a big wooden cupboard and opened the door. She brought out a large burlap bag and handed it to Jack.

"This is for you, young sir," she said smiling. "Now you can go back home to your mother."

Jack set the bag on the table and opened it. An expression of surprise covered his face. The bag was filled with gold.

"I can't take this," Jack protested.

"Yes you can, and you will," the old woman answered. "My late husband, bless his soul, provided well for us. I have more money—enough for me and Clarissa for the rest of our lives. Now you take that money home to your mother."

Jack smiled and glanced at Clarissa. Then he said to the old woman, "I would ask you for something else."

"Go ahead, young sir," the old woman answered.

"I would like your daughter's hand in marriage—that is, if she will have me."

The old woman smiled broadly. "With my blessings, Jack. With my blessings."

Clarissa ran to Jack and threw her arms around him. And as she pressed her lips against his, he knew for certain that everyone concerned would...

...live happily ever after—in spite of the fact that Clarissa never shut up until the day she died!

Imagine running into a ghost—literally!

Here's an example. You have just gone to the closet to find something to wear for the day. After a great deal of searching, you choose something appropriate. Suddenly you have the strange feeling that something is behind you, watching. The hackles on the back of your neck raise. Then you turn around and step right through an apparition that had been lurking behind you. Is the prospect of such an encounter enough to send chill bumps up your back?

One woman in Washington County has had such an experience—and she has had it over and over again. In her house there lived...

The Ghost Who Kept Running into People

There are a lot more burial plots in upper East Tennessee than one might imagine. There are so many, in fact, that all of them will probably never be located. Problems with these lost graveyards arise (pun intended) when houses are unknowingly built over them. When that happens, the ghosts of those buried there are often disturbed and suddenly come forth to pester the living.

A lost graveyard might have been the reason for a haunting when a new house was built on Bayless Road, near Jonesborough, about a quarter century ago.

Public cemeteries are a relatively new concept. Certainly, most churches had private graveyards for members. But more often than not, especially in farming communities like Jonesborough, the dead were buried in family plots located on farms. Regular cemetery lots were just too expensive.

Over the years, these little burial patches fell into neglect. The stones were damaged, and some were carried away by vandals. Grass grew wild and deep. Eventually nothing was left—at least, nothing identifiable to mark a graveyard. Then, as if to deliver a final insult, the family plots were forgotten altogether—just like they never existed.

Then farms were sold and subdivided into building lots. Unsuspecting homeowners built their houses over the graves. Time-honored traditions forbid disturbing the dead. If they are disturbed, they become restless. Therefore, it was not surprising that when the house was completed above, it was often haunted by those buried beneath.

Twenty-five years ago Frances S. and her husband built their dream house about three miles from Jonesborough on Bayless Road, less than a mile from Hairetown Road. From the day they moved into their new home, Frances knew the place was haunted. How? She continually bumped into the resident ghost—literally bumped into him.

"The first few years we were there, I bumped into this 'whatever' constantly," Frances said. "I've walked out of our closet and just ran into someone. And I'd say, 'You scared me to death.' That's how plain he would be."

After her daughters were born, they saw the ghost too. But her husband and son never did. The haunting made one of her daughters so nervous that, to this day, she will not come into the house alone.

Frances's house is a ranch-style dwelling of eight rooms, located on one floor. The haunting seems to center around the foyer. But the ghost has been seen, as well as made its presence known, in every room.

"Our kitchen and den are all one room," Frances said. One night she was standing in the kitchen preparing supper. Suddenly, the hair on the back of her neck stood up straight and she had a strong feeling that something unseen was watching her.

"I looked toward the den," she said. "There was a man standing there. He had long hair. He was standing behind the couch. I knew that part of him had to be stuck in the wall itself because that couch *is up against that wall*."

Frances described her ghost as having long brown hair—shoulder length. Sometimes he wears a red and white checked shirt. He says nothing and makes no other noise when he is visible. Sometimes he appears solid—sometimes not. He appears for only a few seconds, then disappears in the wink of an eye. Frances has absolutely no idea who he is, and she never knows where he's going to pop up next!

"One day I was standing at the foot of my bed," Frances said. "I thought I was talking to one of my children. But when I turned around, *he was there*. I wasn't talking to a child at all, but to a ghost!"

Frances jokingly feels the figure might be her guardian angel because he's constantly underfoot—he's always around. As I said, she keeps bumping into him. At other times she hears only his footsteps walking down the hallway. But when she investigates the noises, nothing is there.

Whether the footsteps actually belong to the ghost of the long-haired man, she's not sure. It might be another ghost—maybe even one of three. There is certainly good reason to believe this may be true.

One day she glanced out her back door just in time to see three "wispy" figures floating across her backyard, through an open field, heading in the general direction of a nearby creek. Frances said she could not tell whether the figures were male, female, or what.

"I'm wondering if we didn't build this house on a burial ground or something," she said with a nervous smile.

Frances told me that she has not seen the ghost of the man for a few years now. "When we first built the house, I used to bump into him all the time. But every time I told someone about the ghost, he would disappear for a month or two, then reappear again. But it seems like he's gone for good now."

One prevalent theory about ghosts is that a haunt has only a limited amount of energy to draw from—like a flashlight bulb from a battery. Ghosts, very active at first, eventually seem to run out of steam. The ghost is seen less and less until, finally, it is seen no more.

This may apply to Frances's ghost. He may have simply run out of energy. Although Frances said she was not afraid of her ghost, she still has had some unnerving experiences with him. And she's been forced to deal with him for a very long time.

Maybe the haunting of her house is finally over, but a quarter of a century can seem like an eternity while waiting for the battery to finally run down.

The ghost of a murdered person often haunts the spot where the crime took place. Sometimes, only the apparition is present. In the following case, however, even more tangible evidence of a heinous crime is evident.

The house where the murder took place has long been torn down. But while it stood, it struck fear in even the stoutest of hearts. Strange noises were heard within. Shadowy apparitions glided through darkened hallways. And one room in the building was both famous and infamous because it contained...

The Ceiling That Dripped Blood

As houses go, the white clapboard structure on Cherokee Street was neither large nor grand. It was, however, infamous. The house had a violent history. In the 1920s a man was alleged to have been murdered in the attic. Up until the time it was torn down, over 60 years ago, the ceiling over the living room periodically dripped blood.

It all began quite innocently. One summer an itinerant salesman had come to town. His Model-T truck was chock-full of goods that he sold to local merchants. There were pots and pans and skillets, small kitchen utensils, bolts of cloth, candy, tools, and notions. Today the salesman would be called a "manufacturer's representative" because he handled the goods of many different manufacturers. He traveled throughout East Tennessee, Southwest Virginia, and Western North Carolina selling his wares.

In the 1920s Jonesborough was a bustling farm community. Once a week, Washington County residents would come to town to purchase supplies or just to stand around on street corners and gossip. The salesman found it easy to sell his goods in town, so by the time he had finished his rounds of local merchants, his wallet had fattened considerably.

But the salesman's success did not escape the notice of the criminal element in Jonesborough, and a certain pair plotted ways they could relieve him of his money. They knew the salesman carried his wad of money with him because he didn't trust banks. They also knew the salesman carried a .45 pistol on him at all times to protect himself.

Late one night, when the salesman was returning from supper at one of the local restaurants, the pair waylaid the man on the darkened street. They relieved him of his weapon, bound and gagged him, and dragged him into the attic of the white-framed house which was, at the time, vacant. There they robbed him of his money and murdered the man in cold blood.

A week later a peculiar odor began drifting from the house. The horrible, sickening smell continued unchecked for several days, because it was assumed that an animal had died underneath the structure. No one wanted to crawl underneath and drag it out. But the odor persisted. A number of citizens lodged complaints, and the Washington County Sheriff was called in to investigate.

It took several more days for the sheriff to arrive at the house. His department was busy investigating the abandonment of the salesman's truck. The vehicle had been found parked on a side street, but the salesman was nowhere to be found. The sheriff suspected foul play.

When the sheriff and his deputy arrived, they found nothing under the house, or around it, that accounted for the stench. Perhaps the smell came from inside. Since the house was empty, they forced the front door open and stepped inside.

The house had not been lived in for years, and a thick layer of dust covered almost everything. Rat droppings littered the floor. The place smelled musty and rank.

Suddenly the deputy gasped and pointed to the ceiling. The sheriff looked up. A blood stain covered about half of it, and blood was dripping down into a puddle on the floor.

The sheriff and his deputy squeezed their way through a tiny passageway into the attic and discovered the body of the salesman. Because it was July and the weather was hot, the corpse was badly decomposed. The stench was overwhelming, and both men, coughing and gasping, fled to the fresh air outside the house.

With much effort, the body was finally removed. The next of kin was notified, and the corpse was shipped home on the next train.

To be perfectly fair about the whole incident, the sheriff tried his level best to discover who had murdered the poor salesman, but the culprits had long gone. They were never captured.

A year passed, and the owner of the house rented it to a newly-wed couple from out of town. The man, a railroad employee, and his bride knew nothing of the sordid goings-on in the house, but trouble started the first night they moved in.

The couple had just gone to sleep when they were aroused by the sound of a man screaming in terror. The husband leaped from the bed and thrust his head out the window. Nothing. The screaming continued.

"It sounds like it's coming from our house," the woman said.

The man turned to her. "Impossible. There's no one here but you and me."

"I don't think so," his wife replied. "Listen."

The screams appeared to be coming from the attic, directly over their heads. The man grabbed a .38 revolver that he kept beside the bed for protection.

"I'm going up in the attic and see what it is," the man announced.

"Be careful," his wife said nervously. Then she pulled the blanket over her head.

Just like the sheriff and his deputy had done one year before, the husband squeezed through the little doorway that led to the attic. It was dark up there. And musty. He could hardly see his gun in front of him.

"Is there anyone here?" he half whispered, half shouted into the gloom. Nothing. No reply. The man pulled the pistol hammer back in anticipation. "I said, *Is there anyone here?* You'd better show yourself. I have a gun."

Still there was no answer. The man searched the attic thoroughly. No one there. After searching every nook and cranny for ten minutes or so, he turned and climbed back down through the hole and returned to the bedroom. He found his wife still in bed with the covers over her head.

Finally she lowered them. Her face was frozen with fear.

"I see you're back again," she said. "I'm sorry. I was so scared. I didn't dare pull the covers down the first time you came back into the room."

"What do you mean 'the first time'?" the man asked in surprise.

"Don't try to scare me," the wife said, her voice quaking. "You came into the room and sat on the bed. Then you went back out again. I'm sorry that I kept the covers over my head the whole time, honey. I was just too scared to put them down."

"I didn't come back into the room," the man said. "I've been in the attic the whole time."

The woman's eyes widened in horror. "If you've been up in the attic.... Heaven help me! **WHAT WAS SITTING WITH ME ON THE BED?!!!!**"

For the rest of the night the husband sat with his wife, his arms around the nearly hysterical woman. They finally fell asleep just before sunrise and slept until ten o'clock. An hour later, they were eating breakfast. Luckily it was a Saturday and the husband could enjoy a day off.

The man was just finishing his coffee when his still nervous wife announced that she was going into the living room to continue unpacking. Her terrified scream brought him running.

He looked up to where she was pointing. A huge pool of blood stained the ceiling and was dripping onto the sofa. Later that afternoon, the couple moved out of the house for good.

The house stood empty for quite some time after that. No one wanted to move in, and the house was becoming a target for vandals and trespassers.

One Halloween night a group of children decided to spend the night in the house. A short time later, they ran hysterically from the premises, screaming at the top of their lungs. And they kept on running until they were in the safety of their own homes.

What had they seen?

One of the children, now a prominent Washington County business-man, said the ghost of the murdered salesman had drifted into the room with the children and panicked everyone. After that, he swore he would never go back in the house again. In fact, as long as the house stood, he gave it a wide berth.

Finally, in the early 1930s, the landlord decided to tear the house down.

Some old-timers in Jonesborough still remember the infamous house that dripped blood. Some have even been inside the house, visiting it as children. But I could find none that ever returned, even after a single visit.

Goblin in the Cellar

This story is a consolidation of a number of tales about a little creature sighted numerous times in upper East Tennessee. Sometimes called a "goblin," sometimes a "demon," the origin of stories about this ugly little creature is the subject of much speculation.

Tales of the goblin are as numerous as that of the so-called "Wampas Cat." I feel the character was invented by pioneer families to frighten their children into staying close to the cabin. After all, there were far more dangerous creatures living in the depths of the forest than the central figure of the following story.

I first heard about the goblin from a man living near Erwin. His family was one of the first to settle on the western slope of the Unaka Mountains in the latter part of the eighteenth century. This man said he heard his grandfather talk about when *his* grandfather met the little creature along the banks of Indian Creek.

Soon afterward, similar stories came to my attention. I printed one of the best of these in my book, <u>Demon In The Woods</u>. And since then, even more stories about a tiny goblin have come to light. I've found the printing of stories like this one triggers half-forgotten memories of stories that were told to us as children. "Yes," readers have told me. "Now I remember my grandfather told me such a tale. And here's what he said...."

Like the mysterious Wampas Cat, said to stalk the forests (and even the cities and towns) of East Tennessee, this enigmatic little creature has been sighted time after time. There seems to be no harm in the creature. But since it resembles Biblical demons, it is often thought to be a minion of the devil. In some versions of the story, it also seems to possess some kind of magical powers.

There have even been accounts of people taking pot shots at these goblins with guns. Some say they can be killed. I understand that one man in Washington County even killed a goblin and stuffed the body. For years, he kept the creature in his living room like a hunting trophy.

The following yarn is not an authentic folktale as such. Rather it contains bits and pieces of the many goblin tales I have heard over the years, assembled to satisfy a personal curiosity. I have often wondered what would happen in the 1990s if someone suddenly discovered and captured one of these creatures in his home.

The wiry little creature rose up on spindly legs and stretched to his full 18-inch height. His cat-like eyes scanned the pale horizon. He tried to get his bearings. But he was more lost than ever.

In the distance a strange animal howled. The creature stopped in his tracks, then ducked behind a rock. He had never heard a sound quite *like that* before.

From far off, he saw a very dim light shining from a building. Perhaps, he thought, he could find shelter there—not only from the strange animal, but from a biting cold that was suddenly sweeping down from the mountains.

Emerging from behind the rock, the creature slowly made his way across the open field. Dry, brown grass crackled under his cloven hooves. He glanced nervously from side to side. Once again, the creature heard the strange howling sound.

The tall grass gave way to shorter, greener stubble. It was easier for the little creature to walk. The structure was much closer now—just a short sprint away. At the base was a large hole. A set of stairs led to an underground room. Perhaps he could hide there for the night.

He had nearly reached the hole when he heard a growling sound behind. He wheeled around and came face to face with a beast, as tall as himself, but much bulkier, covered with short reddish-brown hair.

The creature hunched over, his head lowered, his ears back, his eyes glowing yellow in the dim light. He turned and raced toward the open hole, his pursuer close behind.

Then the little creature felt himself falling. His hoof struck something hard. He tripped and fell again. A few feet away, his enemy pounded behind him. Terror and pain seized the little creature. Then he stopped falling and tried to stand on his own two feet. He limped across the packed dirt and found shelter behind some large boxes. There was a loud crash. The careening red monster plowed into the cardboard. Boxes tumbled on both the pursuer and pursued.

The hole was suddenly bathed in bright light. A deep voice rang out. "Juno, what's the matter with you!"

Heavy footsteps pounded down a set of wooden steps. "Dad blame it, dog, what's going on down there?" the deep voice shouted. "It's the middle of the night."

The big red dog paid no heed. Its attention was focused on the strange little creature cowering in the corner.

More footsteps. The voice was closer this time. "I said, 'what's the matter with you, dog?' " The animal yelped in pain and there were sounds of scuffling. "Stop fighting me, Juno! If I have to drag you out of the cellar by this collar, I will!"

Then the creature heard another voice, this one higher pitched. "What's going on down there, Daddy?"

"Go back to bed, Sean. This worthless hound of yours must have found a rat. That's all. It must've ducked behind these boxes."

Again the dog yelped and struggled to get loose. His rear end crashed into the boxes, sending them into further disarray. The little creature ducked to avoid a heavy corner of one falling on his head.

"Dang it, dog. I told you to hold still!" the man yelled impatiently. Juno began to bark as if there were no tomorrow.

Suddenly, the frayed leather collar around his neck snapped, and the dog broke loose from the man's grip. The animal lunged onto the boxes. The noise was deafening to the terrified little creature. He screamed at the top of his lungs. There was a momentary struggle as the man regained control of the dog.

"What in the name of Pete have you got in there, boy?" the man asked in surprise. "I never heard a rat *scream like that before*. It sounded more like a wildcat."

Finally the little creature could take it no longer. With some difficulty he scrambled from beneath the boxes and ran across the dirt floor. The dog, with the man holding on to the skin on the back of his neck, was in hot pursuit.

"What in heaven's name...?"

Sean Nelson scampered down the steps. The little creature backed into the corner, cowering and shivering in fright. It took most of the man's strength to hold the barking dog back.

"What is it, Daddy?" Sean asked, wide-eyed. "What is that thing?"

John Nelson, who was a government naturalist, couldn't be sure, but he formulated a quick theory. "Don't quote me son, but I'd say that your stupid dog has just scared up a goblin. My daddy told me there was such things, but I didn't believe him." Then Mr. Nelson dropped to his knees and put the struggling dog into a tight headlock.

Juno felt the pressure ease off his neck for a moment and tried to lunge again, but the man was fast and had managed a good grip. "Listen, Juno. We're going to have to get you under wraps until we get this thing figured out. Sean, get that rope in the corner and tie Juno to the post."

After tying up Juno, man and boy returned their attention to the little creature who was still cowering in the corner of their basement. He had been too frightened to run.

"Ugly little thing, ain't he?" Mr. Nelson said to his son.

"Actually, he's kind of cute," Sean replied. "I wonder if he's tame?"

"I'm told that goblins are magic. My grandfather said that. He also said goblins are servants of the devil and are to be avoided at all costs."

"You mean he might put a spell on us—that he might turn us into frogs or something?"

"I reckon that's what Preacher Cox would say about it."

Then Sean edged closer to the creature.

"Careful," his father warned.

The boy stooped down. "Are you really evil?" Sean asked the little creature, just as if he could understand.

The goblin looked up, his cat's eyes blinking. True, he looked just like the pictures of little goblins and demons that Sean had seen in storybooks. His greenish gray skin was pebbled just like a dinosaur's. Mr. Nelson stooped down beside his son and studied the little creature. "Where on earth did you come from, young fella?" he asked. "And even more important, what are you up to?"

"Looks like something between a cat and a bulldog," Sean observed. "Look at those creepy eyes and that underbite—just like the boxer who lives down the road."

"Not to mention the cloven hoofs and the pointed ears," his father added. "Yes, son. We definitely got ourselves a goblin in the cellar. The question is not that we've got it, but what are we going to do with it?"

"I suppose we're going to have to keep him," Sean ventured.

The father turned to his son. "Keep him?" he said, raising his eyebrows. "Sean, this is not a lost puppy. This is a goblin. A real live, bona fide goblin. And he's probably lost."

"Lost from where?" the little boy asked.

The father returned a worried gaze to the little creature and shook his head. "I shudder to think," he answered.

After a moment or two of observation and speculation, Sean held out his hand to the creature. "Come on, fella. Nobody's gonna hurt you."

The father was about to warn his son to be careful, but he was too intrigued with the goblin to say anything. This was a scientist's dream—like finding a real live dinosaur munching leaves in your backyard. If anyone could make friends with this odd creature, his son could. After all, didn't Sean have a wild skunk that visited the farm on occasion, eating scraps out of his son's hand? Sean had a way with animals. Maybe he had a way with goblins, too.

Still tied to the post, Juno lunged as if to protect the boy. But the rope snapped him back suddenly and he yelped in pain. The goblin cowered farther into the corner. Sean smiled. "Don't let him bother you, fella. Juno's all bark." Then he reached out his hand again. The creature hissed like a cat backed into a corner.

Sean drew back his hand a little. He feared he might be too bold and that the creature would suddenly lash out and bite him. After all, there was no telling what kind of diseases the strange creature carried.

Then the goblin stopped his hissing. He studied Sean. Once again, Sean held out his hand and beckoned with his finger. "It's OK, fella," he said gently. "Come on. It's OK."

Sean's father stood up. The goblin reacted to this new move by drawing back a little. "Food might soothe the little beast and make him more friendly," he said. "I'll go to the kitchen and get something. I wonder what goblins like to eat."

"How about a piece of that homemade raisin bread Aunt Madge brought by yesterday," Sean suggested. "He might like something sweet."

"That's as good as anything, I reckon," Sean's father said as he walked up the steps. Then in parting he added, "Be careful with that thing, now. No telling what he might do."

Aunt Madge's homemade raisin bread was known throughout Washington County to be so good that it would satisfy both man and beast. Apparently, goblins also succumbed easily to its charms. Sean needed very little encouragement to entice the goblin to take a hunk of the bread. The goblin then sat on the edge of a small red toolbox, happily munching his bread. Raisins were new to him and he didn't know how to deal with them. They kept getting stuck on the roof of his mouth and in his pointed, needle-sharp teeth. Sean and his father sat on the packed dirt of the cellar floor, in front of their tiny guest, watching him eat.

Mr. Nelson said, "We have us a problem, son. We have to do something with this creature. We can't take him back to where he came from, simply because we don't know where that somewhere is."

"I wonder if there are any more like him at home?" Sean asked.

"Probably. I just wish I knew where 'home' was."

"Maybe he really is from the infernal regions."

John Nelson rubbed the stubble on his chin with the back of his finger and yawned. "Don't think so, son. Don't ask me why, because I can't rightly tell you. But I don't think this little fella has anything to do with the devil."

"Maybe we could ask around."

Sean's father popped a bushy eyebrow into a magnificent arch on his face. Then he looked back at the goblin who was happily finishing off the last crumb of the bread. "And just who would you like me to start off with? The sheriff, perhaps? I can just hear it now. 'Sheriff, we have this goblin who wandered into our cellar last night. He hasn't got any collar or tags. Do you know who he might belong to?' "

Sean scooted closer to the goblin and held out his finger. The goblin gingerly took the end of it with his tiny hand. A smile spread over Sean's face and he turned to his father.

"His hand is warm," Sean said. "I figured it would be cold as ice."

"Preacher Cox would say it is probably a lingering warmth from the infernal regions," his father answered sarcastically.

Sean looked back into the face of the goblin. "I don't think so, Daddy. I don't think this little fellow has anything to do with the devil. I think it's an animal, just like Juno over there. We've just never seen anything like it before."

Sean's father turned to the dog who was tied to a post, his head between his paws, his big brown eyes looking pitiful like he had lost his best friend. Then Mr. Nelson turned back to the goblin.

"I'll tell you what, Sean," he said. "I have a friend—a biology professor over at East Tennessee State University. He was my instructor when I was there. I must admit, I'm a bit curious about our little friend here. Why don't I give him a call and get him to come out for a look. I reckon it wouldn't hurt. Maybe he could come up with some answers."

Sean smiled at the goblin, and the little creature seemed to almost smile back. Calling in an expert was a good idea, Sean thought. At least, the professor would have more answers than either he or his father had right now.

By next morning the goblin had acquired a name—J.W. Just before he dropped off to sleep, Sean had thought it up. The goblin reminded him of his great-uncle J.W. Bishop, who closely resembled a friendly bulldog.

Mr. Nelson gave grudging approval to the name Sean chose. Great-uncle J.W. could not help how he looked. But since the old man lived clear across the other side of the country—in Santa Ana, California— there was little chance he or his namesake would ever meet face to face.

So he would never know that *a goblin had been named after him.*

J.W. had spent a peaceful night in an old cardboard box on Sean's bedroom floor. The little fellow was provided with a folded army surplus blanket for a mattress. Another blanket protected him against the night's chill. A small blue throw cushion from the living room couch served as a pillow.

All through the night, from his bed, Sean glanced nervously to the box where J.W. was sleeping. He was worried that J.W. would wander off. But every time he looked, the little fellow was fast asleep, snoring softly.

In the morning, Sean fed J.W. a slice of buttered toast. Then he offered the little goblin a piece of crisp bacon that his father had fried in a big cast iron skillet. J.W. turned up his nose at the meat—he wouldn't touch it no matter how much he was encouraged to do so.

"I think he only eats vegetables," Mr. Nelson observed wryly.

Since it was Sunday morning, Sean and his father were in the process of getting ready for church. The problem was: what were they going to do with J.W. while they were gone? They couldn't just leave him alone in the house. No telling what might happen.

"I've got an idea," Sean said with a smile on his freckled face. "Why not take him with us."

"I don't think that would be a very good idea," Mr. Nelson answered. "I don't reckon the congregation would take too kindly to us bringing a goblin to church."

Mr. Nelson was right. Preacher Cox was constantly raging from the pulpit about Satan and his evil deeds. Even though there was no evidence that J.W. knew the devil personally, still one had to be careful about what people thought—especially some of the more zealous members of Yorkin Hollow Church of the Redeemer. As Mr. Nelson rightfully observed, *"No matter how you cut it, Sean, J.W. looks exactly like a demon is supposed to look!"*

Sean and his father had attended Yorkin Hollow for the two years since Sean's mother had died in an automobile accident. John Nelson was one of the deacons of the church, a position of responsibility and importance. Yorkin Hollow Church of the Redeemer's pastor, Preacher

Cox, constantly admonished his deacons to hold themselves up as spiritual examples for the rest of the congregation. He certainly wouldn't tolerate it if one of his deacons harbored an alleged goblin.

Against Mr. Nelson's better judgment, however, the decision was made to take J.W. with them as far as the church parking lot but not to let him out of the car once they got there.

Mr. Nelson found an old dog carrier he once used when Juno had to be taken to the vet. It was a large metal box with a wire-covered window at one end. On the door was a latch that accommodated a padlock. Mr. Nelson washed the bottom out carefully with soap and water. Then he laid a clean blanket on the bottom, put J.W. into the box, and closed the wire mesh door. Since he had lost the lock long ago, Mr. Nelson twisted a stiff piece of wire in place to hold the door shut. That would prevent J.W. from escaping.

"Sorry, ol' feller," Mr. Nelson apologized. "I have to keep you under wraps until we can figure out what to do with you. We can't have a goblin running loose all over the countryside."

J.W. looked forlornly through the wire grate and made a little noise that sounded like a bird chirping. Juno looked up and emitted a low growl. Then Mr. Nelson left the room to find out if Sean was ready.

Juno looked up to make sure everything was clear. Then he sidled over to the wire door and sniffed J.W. Mr. Nelson reentered the room and laid a gentle hand on the dog's head, patting him gently.

"That's OK, boy," he said to J.W. "I don't reckon he'll hurt you."

J.W. reached out with a three-fingered hand and touched the dog's nose. Juno yelped and drew back. After he had recovered from the initial shock, Juno approached the box again and sniffed. J.W. reached out again, and this time Juno didn't jump back.

Mr. Nelson scratched his head. "Sean, look at this," he called to his son, who was just finishing dressing for church in his own bedroom. "That goblin is patting Juno on the muzzle. And the darned-fool dog likes it!"

J.W. chirped like a bird, immensely satisfied with himself.

The Yorkin Hollow Church of the Redeemer was only a short drive down Embreeville Road. By the time Sean and his father arrived, the sexton was ringing the final bell, calling the congregation to worship. Before leaving the car, Mr. Nelson rolled down the back window so J.W. could get some air.

The church building was small—built of whitewashed cinder block. Inside, ten rows of plain wooden pews faced a handmade pulpit. On the far wall, a six-foot wooden cross, made of weathered barn wood, hung behind the preacher. To the right, a wheezy reed organ provided an uncertain accompaniment to hymns. Eight bare bulbs overhead provided light. There was no Sunday School building, and the only bathrooms were outside—one small cinder block building for the men and one for the women.

Most of the congregation was already seated when Sean and his father found their usual places in the back pew—the "Amen corner," as Mr. Nelson liked to call it. The back pew was a safe place to be once the "hallelujahs" began in earnest.

Mr. Nelson liked the people in Yorkin Hollow—hardworking, plain people with a straightforward attitude about their faith. They took the Scripture at face value. What the Bible said was law—that was all there was to it! Although he didn't agree with everything that happened in the church, he and Sean attended every Sunday without fail.

The service began when the song leader—a young chap by the name of Mason Dandy—announced that "Blood of the Lamb" would be the first hymn. The congregation was small, but their lusty singing—once it got wound up—could be heard a half-mile down the road. A rousing camp meeting song like "Blood of the Lamb" could be heard as far away as Gilbert Perkins's dairy farm, located just on the other side of the creek.

(Gil Perkins never went to church. He claimed he could sit on his front porch and get all the religion he needed by listening to the singing up the road. He claimed that when the weather was right, he could even hear the preaching. Mr. Perkins's allegedly heathen ways were looked down upon by many of the faithful in Washington County. But Sean regarded him as one of his best friends. Besides, no one could pull a hornyhead out of the creek like Mr. Perkins. He knew all the right places to fish—something that he did often and well.)

The second hymn the congregation sang was the ever-popular "Amazing Grace." Hardly a Sunday passed without the singing of "Amazing Grace" at least once—maybe even twice—during the service. Even so solemn a hymn as "Amazing Grace" was sung like a camp meeting song.

The third hymn was "What a Friend We Have in Jesus."

When the singing finally stopped, Preacher Cox, a red-faced, white-haired, and loud-voiced clergyman, took his place behind the pulpit. He whapped his hand down heavily on the large Bible, looked heavenward, rolled his eyes, and said, "Let us pray."

The only thing that seemed longer than Preacher Cox's sermons were Preacher Cox's prayers. Some lasted 20 minutes or more. This morning was no exception. Just when you thought he had run out of people to pray for, he would think of someone else. And since it was not considered good manners to fidget around or leave the church hall when Preacher Cox was addressing the Almighty, a few of the congregation always departed immediately after the final "Amen" to visit one of the two outhouses behind the church.

Today Amanda Bundy was the first to leave, followed closely by Hank Thomas.

Mrs. Bundy was a good-hearted soul who had lost her husband years before when he was crushed to death by a toppling tractor. Fortunately, Mr. Bundy had left his wife a sizable farm and a few thousand dollars that he had stuffed away in an old pillow. His grown son Mike took over the day-to-day operation of the farm, leaving Mrs. Bundy free to pursue her favorite pastime—cooking for the neighborhood.

No one ever went hungry in Washington County as long as Mrs. Bundy could stand before her stove and cook. Indeed, Mrs. Bundy was a living saint and a cornerstone of Yorkin Hollow Church of the Redeemer.

Suddenly, the congregation heard a horrified scream from outside. Then Hank Thomas burst through the door to announce breathlessly that Mrs. Bundy had fainted dead away on the parking lot.

Preacher Cox was the first to arrive at the side of the prostrate woman. She was just coming to, and her eyes snapped open in wild-eyed horror.

"Get it away," she screamed. "Get it away! Don't let it get me!"

"Get *what* away, Amanda?" the preacher asked, patting her hand.

"The demon," she replied breathlessly. "There's a demon in this parking lot. It tried to get me."

The rest of the congregation, which had gathered in a circle, looked around and murmured to themselves.

"There's nothing here, Amanda," Preacher Cox replied.

Mrs. Bundy struggled to a sitting position. "Don't tell me there ain't nothing here, Preacher," she said angrily. "I saw him myself. I was on my way back to the church when I saw him staring at me from underneath one of the cars."

Sean and his father, standing behind the rest of the congregation, looked at each other uneasily. J.W. must have gotten loose somehow, and there was no telling where he was now.

Trying not to attract attention, Mr. Nelson slowly made his way to the car and looked in the backseat. The box was still there and J.W. was still inside, looking as sorrowful as ever. Mr. Nelson motioned to Sean to hurry to the car.

Preacher Cox gasped for air as he tried to pull the immensely overweight Mrs. Bundy to her feet. She was clearly frightened and looked around the parking lot nervously. Preacher Cox steadied her with his hand.

Mrs. Bundy turned to the preacher. "Well, what are you going to do about this?" she asked indignantly, her eyes flashing.

The preacher smiled tolerantly. "Amanda, did you really see a demon?"

Amanda Bundy jerked from his grasp, her eyes flashing with indignation. "Of course I did. You calling me a liar?"

"Now calm down, Amanda. Just where did you see this thing?"

Mrs. Bundy frowned. "I told you. Underneath one of the cars."

"Which car, Amanda?"

Amanda Bundy looked around just in time to see Mr. Nelson's red Ford Ranger easing out of the parking lot. She pointed a chubby finger toward the departing vehicle. "That one. John Nelson's."

Preacher Cox squinted into the distance. The Ford pulled out onto Yorkin Hollow Road, then disappeared around a curve. He turned to Mrs. Bundy.

"Are you sure you saw the demon under Brother Nelson's car?" he asked again, this time very seriously.

"Yes I did," Mrs. Bundy replied. "And may God strike me down if I'm lying."

Preacher Cox frowned. Amanda Bundy was not the kind of person to lie—especially in Scriptural matters. And dealings with the devil definitely fell into that category as far as Preacher Cox was concerned. If Amanda said she saw a demon, *then she saw a demon.* There was just no question about her judgment in such matters!

Then the preacher scratched his head. What was John Nelson up to? Well, he was determined to find out—and as quickly as possible.

As was their custom after church, Sean and his father ate lunch at Gayle's Restaurant on U.S. 11-E, just outside Jonesborough. Sean had a hot dog and french fries. Mr. Nelson ate his usual hamburger steak plate. Then he ordered a salad to go—no dressing. That was for J.W.

Back home, Mr. Nelson wondered out loud how Amanda Bundy had seen J.W. peering at her from underneath the car when he was clearly still in the box. Was J.W., in fact, really a goblin? Was he really magic? Could he disappear from one place and reappear in another?

Mr. Nelson placed a call to his friend at ETSU and suggested that he come out right away.

"It's Sunday afternoon," came the reply on the other end of the phone. "I promised the wife I'd take her over to the mall to do some shopping."

"Listen, Sam," Mr. Nelson protested. "We have this little emergency over here. We've found this.... Well, we have this animal. We need you to take a look at him for us."

"Why the rush?"

Mr. Nelson hesitated for a moment, looking for the right words to say.

"Listen, just do me this favor," Mr. Nelson replied finally. "Trust me. I know you won't be disappointed."

An hour later, Dr. Sam Thomas stood at the Nelsons' door waiting to come into the house.

John Nelson shook his hand and asked him to come inside. "Sam, am I ever glad to see you. Thanks for coming."

Dr. Thomas scowled. "You realize that my wife is extremely mad at both of us, John. What's so important about this animal that I have to identify it right away? You're a hotshot government naturalist. You've had enough biology and zoology. Don't you know what it is?"

Just then, the two men were joined by Sean. Mr. Nelson said, "You remember my son, Sean, don't you?"

Dr. Thomas smiled and extended his hand. The old man's ruddy complexion contrasted sharply with his snow-white hair, white bushy eyebrows, and pale blue eyes. "Glad to see you again, young man," he said pleasantly.

Then Mr. Nelson said, "Sean, go get J.W."

Sean left the room and appeared a few seconds later with something wrapped up in a brown towel like a newborn infant. He set the towel down on the kitchen table and unwrapped it. Slowly, J.W. stood up and blinked his cat-like eyes at Dr. Thomas. The old professor stared at J.W. for a moment. Then, his voice shaking, he said, "I think I need to sit down."

Mr. Nelson slid a chair under Dr. Thomas's ample backside, and he dropped into it, still staring at J.W. The little goblin chirped and slowly walked over to the old man. Then he, too, sat down on top of the table—squatted down and sat like an Indian at a pow wow.

For several minutes the two stared at each other. Then Dr. Thomas said, "I never thought I'd see the day.... I've heard of these, but...."

"What do you think it is?" Mr. Nelson asked, plopping into a chair beside his old college professor.

The old man shook his head. "I don't know for sure. I mean.... Well, I've heard creatures like this existed, but only in nightmares, or in the horror stories kids tell around the campfire. But I didn't think they really existed. How did you come by this?"

"He came to us, Dr. Thomas," Sean answered. "We found him last night in the cellar. Juno, my dog, cornered him under some boxes. He was scared—at least, he didn't try to fight back."

"Then it's safe to assume this is a basically friendly creature?"

"Yes sir. We even named him J.W."

"I see," Dr. Thomas said. Then he pointed his index finger at J.W. The little goblin chirped and extended his hand, holding on to the end of Dr. Thomas's finger with his three tiny fingers.

"His hand is warm," Dr. Thomas observed. "This creature.... Ahhh, J.W.... J.W. is a warm-blooded animal." Then he smiled at the creature, and J.W. almost seemed to smile back. "And I wouldn't doubt that he's smart, too."

"How smart?" Mr. Nelson asked.

"Well, let's see."

Dr. Thomas reached into his pocket and drew out three nickels. He placed them in front of J.W. "Go ahead, J.W.," the professor said. "Pick them up and look them over."

J.W. turned each coin over with ease, studying each side intently. The professor turned to Mr. Nelson. "Look, John," he said. "J.W. has a flexible thumb—at least a finger that acts as a thumb. That's why he can pick up the coins. Only humans have a flexible thumb. Even chimpanzees have a difficult time picking up small objects from a flat surface."

Then Dr. Thomas turned back to J.W. "Now, young man, let's see how fast you can learn."

Dr. Thomas replaced the coins in front of J.W.—one was heads up, two were tails up. Then, as J.W. watched intently, the professor turned the coins until they were all heads up. J.W. chirped. The professor once more turned the coins until one was heads up and the other two were tails up. Then he sat back in his chair and waited for J.W. to make his move.

J.W. looked at the professor, then he looked back at the coins in front of him. He reached out for the two coins that were tails up and turned them over. In short order, all three coins were heads up. Then he chirped. Mr. Nelson and his son exchanged surprised glances. Dr. Thomas turned to them.

"Now don't jump to conclusions, you two. It could have been a fluke. Let's see if he does it again."

Once again Dr. Thomas turned the coins, and again J.W. had all three heads up. He chirped again.

Dr. Thomas pushed his chair away from the table and chuckled. "Well, boys. I think your little friend, here, is more than just another pretty face. He has brains, too." Then he added, "After this revelation, I need a cup of coffee."

Mr. Nelson brewed two large brown mugs of instant coffee—one for himself and one for the professor. Then he poured Sean a tall glass of cherry Kool-Aid.

When they had settled themselves back around the table, Mr. Nelson asked, "Well, Dr. Thomas. In your professional opinion, what do we have here?"

Dr. Thomas took a sip of his coffee and looked at J.W., who was still sitting cross-legged in the middle of the kitchen table, peacefully munching a carrot. "John, you've heard stories about Old World fairies, brownies, and sprites?"

"You mean folklore."

"Yes," the old man replied thoughtfully. "Every country has its folklore about such creatures. Scientists and other so-called intelligent people dismiss the stories as myth. Remember the story about the shoemaker and the elves?"

"I do," Sean chimed in.

The professor smiled. "Well, young man, what do you want to bet that J.W. here would be able to repair a pair of shoes if called upon to do so?"

"But," John Nelson protested, "how come nobody's ever seen these creatures until now?"

"On the contrary, John. People *have* seen them. How do you think the stories got started in the first place? A person is walking in the woods and comes upon one of them. Then he tells others about the encounter. Before you know it, the whole countryside knows. And now that I've met J.W., I'm also inclined to believe in Bigfoot and the Loch Ness Monster, too. If J.W. can exist, why can't they?"

Dr. Thomas took another sip of his coffee to clear his throat, and Sean asked, "Is J.W. a magical creature? I mean fairies are supposed to be able to put spells on people."

"That's a very good question, Sean, but I don't think so. J.W. is definitely a flesh-and-blood creature, highly intelligent, but not magical. But he's smart enough to make you think so."

Then Sean remembered the incident after church earlier in the day. He told Dr. Thomas what had happened—when J.W. had suddenly appeared underneath the car. Amanda Bundy had seen him and fainted on the spot. How had he gotten out of the dog carrier, then gotten back in again?

"I'll bet that he untwisted those wires to get out," Dr. Thomas replied. "Then after Mrs. Bundy screamed and fainted, he crawled back through the open car window and into the dog carrier, then twisted the wires back." The professor turned to J.W., who was just finishing his second carrot. "Isn't that the way it happened, young man?"

J.W. chirped in reply.

"I thought so," Dr. Thomas laughed. Then he became serious. "There's still one thing I can't figure out. Where did you come from, and are there more at home like you?"

Mr. Nelson scratched his chin. "There would have to be," he said. "If J.W. is a flesh-and-blood creature, he would have to have a mother and father—and probably brothers and sisters. Can you imagine thousands of these things running around?"

"And," Dr. Thomas continued, "is J.W. as big as they get? I have no idea how old he is. Is he just a baby, or is he an adult?"

"I have a question, too," Sean said as he finished the rest of his cherry Kool-Aid. "What are we going to do with him now that we've got him?"

"Well, I'll tell you what I should do," Dr. Thomas said, "but you or J.W. wouldn't like it. Not only would my colleagues like to get a gander at J.W., but he would probably end up on a dissecting table. A very inglorious fate for such a glorious scientific find. But as you know, John, science lacks sentimentality."

A smile lit up Sean's face. "Then we can keep him, Daddy?"

"I reckon we're going to have to," Mr. Nelson answered. "But we can't tell anyone that he's here. I don't think anyone would understand."

The sound of a car pulling up in the gravel driveway distracted them. Sean ran to the window and looked out. Juno began to bark wildly.

"Who is it?" Mr. Nelson asked.

"Batten down the hatches," Sean answered, his voice rising in excitement. "Preacher Cox just drove up in his Cadillac."

There was a wild scramble when Sean, his father, and Professor Thomas frantically searched for a place to hide J.W. from Preacher Cox. It was quickly decided that an empty kitchen cabinet was the safest place for the time being. Dr. Thomas and Sean volunteered to stay in the kitchen with J.W. until the preacher was gone.

Mr. Nelson answered the door. "Reverend Cox. What a surprise to see you."

Preacher Cox said nothing, but briskly walked into the living room and removed his hat. He glanced around the room before he spoke.

"I was in the neighborhood, Brother Nelson, and thought I'd drop in. I've been wanting to talk to you about a matter that's been troubling my spirit. The Lord has directed me to speak to you about it."

"Have a seat, Preacher," Mr. Nelson offered nervously.

"Thank you," the preacher answered, eyeing his host suspiciously. Then he dropped into the softest chair available. Mr. Nelson sat on the couch opposite the preacher and said, "Can I offer you something to drink?"

"No thank you," Preacher Cox replied stiffly. Then he said, "I want to talk to you about that little incident after church this morning with Sister Bundy and your sudden departure from the parking lot. She said she spotted a demon underneath your car."

Mr. Nelson chuckled nervously. "I fear Sister Bundy might have been a little too full of your preaching, Reverend."

"Indeed!" Preacher Cox sniffed. He was not amused. "This matter is not to be taken lightly, Brother Nelson. Sister Bundy was convinced that she saw the demon. As you know, Satan often sends his minions to earth to deceive the faithful."

"I know that, Preacher. I've heard you say it many times."

"Then, may I ask why you left the church so suddenly just after the incident with Sister Bundy?"

John Nelson frowned so Preacher Cox could not possibly miss his displeasure at such a question. "Sean was sick. I wanted to get him home to give him some medicine."

Preacher Cox sat back in the chair and crossed his legs. "I see. Well, for your information, someone saw you and your son eating lunch at

Gayle's Restaurant soon after the incident. It doesn't sound to me like the lad was very sick."

"Feed a cold and starve a fever, Reverend Cox."

The preacher frowned. "And thou shalt not bear false witness, Brother Nelson."

What could Mr. Nelson say? He should have known that in a small town like Jonesborough, someone he knew was bound to see him. All that Preacher Cox had to do was to ask around. In Jonesborough, everybody knew everybody.

Preacher Cox continued: "See here, Brother Nelson. What do you know about this incident you're not telling me?"

The conversation was suddenly interrupted by a clattering in the kitchen—then shouts from Dr. Thomas and Sean. Preacher Cox sat upright in his chair and turned his head toward the noise. John Nelson stood up and started to go toward the kitchen, but he suddenly stopped. He slowly turned and returned to his seat.

Preacher Cox raised his eyebrows. "Aren't you going to investigate that noise?"

"It's just Sean," Mr. Nelson answered nervously. "One of his friends came over and I guess they just knocked over something."

"A friend?" the preacher asked. "I thought you said Sean was sick."

John Nelson didn't have a chance to answer. J.W. ran screaming across the living room floor, with Dr. Thomas and Sean in hot pursuit. Preacher Cox jumped up on the chair when J.W., in headlong flight, ran over his shoes.

"Lord have mercy!" the preacher shouted. "It *is* a demon!" Then he fell over the back of the chair and landed heavily on the floor. He scrambled to his feet just as J.W. wheeled around and headed back toward the kitchen. "Satan is in this house!" he screamed.

"No such thing!" John Nelson shouted back.

Dr. Thomas and Sean ran back through the kitchen, hot on the heels of J.W. Then the back door slammed. Preacher Cox wheeled around and headed for the front door. "I'm going to get my gun," he shouted. Mr. Nelson grabbed him by his coat sleeve.

"J.W. is no devil, Preacher. He's a species of animal that few people have ever seen before. But that's all he is. He's just an animal."

The fear was clearly showing in Preacher Cox's eyes. He pulled loose from Mr. Nelson's grip. "I don't care what you say, Brother Nelson. That thing *is* a devil. He even *looks* like a devil."

Then Preacher Cox opened the screen door and looked back at John Nelson. "I'm going home and get my shotgun and make some telephone calls. I'm going to get as many people as I can to help me, and we're going to track down this servant of Satan and destroy him." Then as an afterthought, Preacher Cox added, "And I wouldn't be getting in our way, Brother Nelson! That could be very dangerous."

J.W. was nearly out of breath. He had breached the short grass of the lawn and now found himself over his head in a new kind of grass. Behind him, he could hear Sean and Dr. Thomas's footsteps. They were getting closer. He couldn't understand why they had shut him up in the dark place in the kitchen. Now that he was finally free, he didn't intend to go back—ever. He would continue running and find a safer place to hide.

Then J.W. heard another sound—a roaring noise that approached much faster than the footsteps. Then he heard a high squeal and a scrunching of rocks. He recognized the sound. It was a vehicle—the same kind that he had ridden in earlier in the day. He ducked behind a boulder. He would wait until the vehicle left.

John Nelson skidded to a halt in a cloud of dust. Sean and Dr. Thomas stopped in their tracks and turned around.

"Any sign of him?" Mr. Nelson asked as he ran toward them.

"No," Professor Thomas said, placing his hands on his knees and gasping for air. He had run quite some distance.

"Are you all right, Sam?" Mr. Nelson asked.

"Yeah. I think so," the professor sputtered between gasps for air. "But I'm getting too old to be running around the countryside looking for runaway goblins." Then he added, "Where's the preacher?"

"He's gone to get his gun and round up a posse. He's bound and determined to shoot J.W. on sight."

"Daddy," Sean said, clearly panicked. "We have to find J.W. before he does."

Mr. Nelson squinted into the late afternoon sunlight that splashed on the newly green hayfield. "It's going to be dark in a few hours. Then we'll never find him." Then he turned to Dr. Thomas and Sean. "By the way, what happened back there in the house. What made J.W. take off like that?"

"Don't know," Dr. Thomas answered. "He was perfectly fine when we put him in the cabinet. Suddenly he burst out of there like all Hades was after him and proceeded to lead us on a merry chase through the house."

Mr. Nelson cupped his hands to his mouth and shouted, "J.W. Where are you, boy. Come on back." He put his hands down for a moment, and all three listened—listened for that tell-tale chirping. But they heard nothing. Mr. Nelson shouted again, "J.W."

Again there was no sound other than the whisper of a light breeze rustling through the hayfield. Mr. Nelson ran his fingers through his hair. "He's got to be in this field somewhere. He's hiding—afraid to come out. Something must have really frightened him, and I don't think it was the preacher."

It took no time at all for Preacher Cox to round up six or seven men, all armed to the teeth. The preacher took down his own 12-gauge shotgun from the shelf. It was an ancient artillery piece that had once belonged to his father. Preacher Cox hadn't used it in years. He found some shells in a dresser drawer and loaded the weapon. Then he got into his Cadillac and headed for U.S. 11-E where he was to meet his posse.

By seven o'clock the caravan of five cars pulled to the side of the road near John Nelson's house. The posse gathered around the preacher.

"He's out there somewhere, boys," the preacher told them. "We've got to work fast. Night's falling. Be careful. This creature's of the devil. No telling what he might do. Shoot first and ask questions later."

Then the men spread out into the field beside the road. They walked along slowly, studying the ground for any sign of cloven hoof prints. But the new growth was already pretty well along, and it was hard to see the dirt.

Just then, Preacher Cox looked up and saw three figures on the other side of the field. He recognized Brother Nelson, Sean, and that heathen professor from State. He turned to the man walking next to him.

"There's Brother Nelson," the preacher said. "He's the one who brought that devil into our midst."

"Want us to take care of him, Preacher?" the man asked, his finger curling around the trigger of his 30-30 rifle.

Preacher Cox frowned. "Not just yet. There'll be time to reckon with him later. Right now we have to find that minion of hell."

Sean halted in mid-step and listened carefully. Had he just heard J.W.'s distinctive chirp? In the meantime, his father and Dr. Thomas glanced uneasily at the armed men searching the other end of the hayfield. "Looks like your friend is serious about gunning down J.W.," the professor observed uneasily.

"Yeah," Mr. Nelson said. "I knew he was a little bit crazy, but not this crazy." Then Mr. Nelson glanced at Sean. "Son, this is liable to get serious out here. I think you'd better go on back to the house and wait until I get there."

Sean ignored his father's warning. "He's around here, Daddy. I thought I heard him."

"Where?"

"Over there by that stand of trees."

Mr. Nelson looked into the distance. A thick clump of woods stood at the end of the hayfield, about 100 yards in front of them. Sean began walking toward the trees. "J.W.," he called softly so he would not arouse the suspicions of the men with the guns. Mr. Nelson and Dr. Thomas began following.

When they were about halfway there, Preacher Cox looked up and noticed the three heading for the trees. He turned to the man next to him. "Brother, I think they've found that devil. Let's go."

Preacher Cox's party reached the Nelsons and Dr. Thomas at the edge of the trees. Mr. Nelson grabbed Preacher Cox's coat and pulled him back. The other men turned and pointed their rifles at Mr. Nelson. Sean

Nelson rushed up and threw his arms around his father's waist in an effort to protect him. Preacher Cox jerked loose from Nelson's grip.

"You will not interfere, John Nelson," Preacher Cox said angrily. "We have been led here to destroy Satan's work. And we intend to do just that."

"You are a sanctimonious idiot, Preacher," Mr. Nelson shouted back. "J.W. is not a creature of the devil. He's just an animal—and a very intelligent one. But you're willing to blow him away just because you don't understand him."

"Hold those guns on him boys," Preacher Cox said. "If he moves, shoot him."

Suddenly, one of the men looked toward a little clearing in the woods and gasped. There in the middle stood J.W., calmly watching the proceedings. All rifles turned toward the little creature.

Then the strangest thing happened. The posse could have shot J.W. easily. They were within point-blank range. But no one pulled a trigger. They just stared at him wild-eyed.

"Shoot, you idiots!" the preacher screamed. No one did. "I said SHOOT!" Still no one pulled a trigger. They were frozen in their tracks.

Preacher Cox turned back to J.W. But this time, the little creature was not alone. He had been joined by another of his kind—this one bigger, much bigger.

"Saints be with us!" Dr. Thomas gasped. "J.W. is only a baby! I'll lay you odds that we're about to meet his daddy."

The newly arrived creature was about five feet tall and, except for its size, looked exactly like J.W. It stood there, glaring at the men. Then it walked over to Preacher Cox and calmly took the shotgun from his hands.

"D-d-don't hurt me," the preacher stammered.

The creature looked at the gun. Then it looked back at Preacher Cox. It hissed softly and put the loaded gun back in the preacher's hand. But Preacher Cox made no attempt to raise his weapon.

Then the creature turned and walked back to J.W. For a few seconds, the two animals chirped at each other—just like they were talking. Then J.W. walked over to where Sean, Mr. Nelson, and Dr. Thomas were standing. Sean stooped down.

"This looks like goodbye, young fellow," Sean said sadly. J.W. nodded his head and chirped. Sean held out his hand and J.W. took it. Then J.W. walked over to Mr. Nelson.

"J.W.," he said. "I can't say it was a total pleasure to make your acquaintance. After all, you did cause quite an uproar. But I'm really going to miss you."

J.W. chirped again.

Dr. Thomas could only shake his head and smile sheepishly. The greatest scientific find of the century was about to walk away from him, and there was nothing he could do about it.

Then J.W. walked back to the bigger goblin. Both disappeared into the woods.

Mr. Nelson, Sean, and Dr. Thomas glanced at each other. Then they looked at Preacher Cox and the other men with rifles, who were just regaining their senses.

"What happened?" they asked each other. But Preacher Cox said nothing. Instead, he turned and began walking slowly across the field toward his car. His posse followed him.

Sean looked up at his father. "Daddy, will we ever see J.W. again?"

John Nelson put a burly hand on his son's shoulder. "I really don't know, son," he answered. Then he looked up at Preacher Cox's retreating figure. "But I know one thing for sure. The preacher's going to have to write a brand new sermon after this."